ARRESTED DEVELOPMENT

AND

PHILOSOPHY

Lyndsey McNeal,

Happy birthday! You're 22. It's a birthday of 2's. In two weeks we get married. Isn't it so hard to believe? It feels like everything is changing. I feel like God gave us each other to be constants in change. There's so much of life yet to come, but we've already been through so much. We're alive, stronger, more deeply in love —so much grace. I can't wait to grow together. I can't wait to spend many more birthdays with you.

Always yours,

Robert Daniel

The Blackwell Philosophy and Pop Culture Series
Series Editor: William Irwin

ARRESTED DEVELOPMENT

AND

PHILOSOPHY

THEY'VE MADE A HUGE MISTAKE

Edited by Kristopher Phillips
and J. Jeremy Wisnewski

WILEY

John Wiley & Sons, Inc.

CONTENTS

PART FIVE
SOLID AS IRAQ: POLITICS AND ETHICS ARRESTED

PART SIX
AND ON THE EPILOGUE . . .

ACKNOWLEDGMENTS

And Now a Few Words from the New CEOs of the Bluth Company

Three years ago we set out to keep this family together . . . and it looks as if . . . (pardon us if we get a bit choked up here) it looks as if we've succeeded in that goal. Okay, maybe we're not really the CEOs of any company, and we certainly didn't succeed in keeping the Bluths on television, let alone together, but we do have some people to thank for making this book happen.

We really lucked out a number of times and would like to extend serious thanks to our Banana Stand staff both for moving the Bluth Company down one floor to save on costs and ultimately saving the company, and for contributing wonderful works to our book without having made too many huge mistakes. We're also endlessly grateful to Connie Santistiban for making this work sparkle, and Bill Irwin for his Michael-esque patience in working with Kris's (very) Buster-esque pestering (panic attacks and all) about the viability of the project.

Kris would like to thank Shawn Akbar and Amber Griffioen for their help and encouragement; you guys are the Gob and Lindsay to his Buster. He would also like to thank various co-graduate students at the U of I for reading papers and giving him invaluable feedback, in particular Seth Jones, Sam Taylor, and Matt Drabek. Kris would also like to extend thanks to his parents Jeff and Joyce Phillips, mostly for being nothing like George Sr. and Lucille, and by that he means, for encouraging him every step of the way. Most importantly, he would like to thank his wife Nateasa McGuire for reading, re-reading, and listening to him read the papers in this book, for giving him ideas much better than those that he came up with himself, and for all of your support.

Jeremy would like to thank Jackie Seamon for reading through the book, hunting out mistakes, and then yelling about them. He would also like to thank all of those friends who listened to him recite scenes from episodes of *Arrested Development*, patiently smiling, and indulging him despite the oodles of other things they had to do. You know who you are. Finally, Jeremy would like to thank his wife, Dorothy, for her continuous support. He wouldn't make it without her. The children also deserve a thank you. It ain't easy being a philosopher's kid—so thanks are due to Audrey and Lucian.

Of course, frozen bananas dipped in chocolate deserve the most thanks of all. When things get rough, after all, there's always money in the Banana Stand.

INTRODUCTION

Kristopher Phillips

This is the story of a wealthy family who lost everything (including their show) and the group of philosophers who had no choice but to write a book about it.

Well, it's a matter of philosophical debate whether or not we really *had* a choice in the matter (or ever), but one thing is for sure—we really wanted to.

The reasons for wanting to write on the philosophical underpinnings in *Arrested Development* are probably as diverse as the characters in the show—I, for one, had many different reasons, including (and certainly not limited to) an intense desire to watch and rewatch the entire series with friends and professors. As I watched, and rewatched, I found myself wondering whether the Bluths really are as unrelatable as they think they are (at least in the third season).

As I watched Buster, the youngest of the Bluth boys and the self-proclaimed "scholar" of the family, it occurred to me that perhaps the show ended prematurely not because the family is weird and difficult to relate to, but rather because each character might be seen to exhibit the traits that we are afraid ("fear turns to anger . . . so frightened inmate number 2 isn't frightened at all, he's a crabby old coot!") that we exhibit in the various roles we fill. For example, I often fear that Buster represents academics in general (or at least perpetual graduate students), especially those of us that tend to study the more esoteric—heady—topics. Buster is someone who is "moderately intelligent" and uses his family's considerable assets to pursue academic avenues that—well, let's face it—really don't offer much by way of preparation for the real world; didn't everything get mapped out by Magellan, or NASA? Buster's life embodies the spirit of the question most often asked to students of philosophy: "What are you going to do with that?"

And Buster is not alone in representing what academics might fear about themselves; just take a look at Tobias. *Qua* (in the role of) academic, Tobias has an impressive resume: He "was chief resident of psychiatry at Mass General for two years and did [his] fellowship in psycholinguistics at MIT." Not too shabby. Not to mention the fact that he was both a practicing therapist and a practicing analyst—a professional twice over . . . but the business cards almost got him arrested, and with good reason! Tobias engenders the old archetype of the academic who is so well educated that he just doesn't really know how to be a real person; he lacks common sense entirely, which might explain the "analrapist" business cards, and the administering of CPR to a sleeping (but healthy) tourist. The traits he embodies, when we look at him as an academic, make him an exaggeration of those fears that academics may have—the total loss of ability to relate to anyone else, complete failure to function in the world, and so on, and all for the cost of an impressive academic resume.

While it's not always obvious how some academic pursuits prepare their scholars for the real world, surprising and extenuating circumstances do pop up.[1] I am optimistic that even if the principles of seventeenth century agrarian business don't quite apply to the housing development business today (we're not too concerned about any uprisings . . . are we?), by the end of this book, the philosophers who contributed to it will have convinced you that the principles of seventeenth-century *philosophy* (and those that are "much, much . . . MUCH older") really do apply to everyday life in the O.C. (don't call it that)—as well as to life in general. Besides being relevant to everyday life, philosophy might even be able to help prevent you from emulating Gob—that is, we might even help you to avoid making "a huge mistake."

NOTE

1. Who would have guessed that a philosophy education could be used to edit a book on the Bluths?

PART ONE

FAMILY FIRST

IS THE EXAMINED LIFE A HUGE MISTAKE?

Happiness, Self-Knowledge, and the Bluths

Jason Southworth and Ruth Tallman

Ignorance is bliss—or is it? While you hear that little nugget of folk wisdom fairly often, some people desire the truth regardless of the repercussions. On the side of ignorance, George Michael decides not to tell Maeby that she's adopted (she's really not) because he thinks she is happier believing she is her parents' biological child.[1] Michael chooses not to tell George Michael that he slept with his ethics teacher (after George Michael professed his love for Ms. Barely), because George Michael is happier not knowing.[2] Yet, on the side of truth, George Sr. escapes from a Mexican prison only to go home to verify his wife's relationship with his brother.[3] So what makes us happier, ignorance or knowledge?

For centuries, analrapists and philosophers have come down on the side of knowledge. I mean, we philosophers *really* need to know the truth (about everything!); we need to know so badly that we even need you to need to know. If you don't, we're unhappy. On the other side of the debate is. . . basically everyone else. Sure, when we're feeling uncharitable we'll point to the MR. Fs and "moron jocks" (Steve Holt (!)) who prefer ignorance, but when we're being fair, philosophers will admit that there are plenty of smart people who seem to think we're wrong about self-knowledge being the key to happiness. Since there are no smart people on television, let's take the Bluths as our guides in reconsidering whether ignorance really is bliss.

The Life of *Arrested Development* Is Not Worth Living

Plato (428/427 BCE–348/347 BCE) is the most famous proponent of the view that self-awareness is the hallmark of a happy person. In his account of the trial and death of his mentor, Socrates (c. 469 BCE–399 BCE), Plato depicts a man who thought pursuing the truth about himself, others, and the world was the most important thing anybody could ever do—indeed, that it was worth dying for (would any member of the Bluth family do that?). Socrates spent his life trying to convince those around him to reflect on their lives and on their values, and to think critically about the kinds of people they were. This comes through clearly in his rebuke of the accusers at his trial: "Are you not ashamed that you give your attention to acquiring as much money as possible, and similarly with reputation and honour, and give no attention or thought to truth and understanding and the perfection of your soul?"[4]

Socrates's actions made him an enemy of many in Athens (no one likes to be told they're behaving badly). Despite the lack of support, and outright hostility of many, Socrates continued to reflect on his own life and urged others to do the same, saying, "Examining both myself and others is really the very best thing that a man can do, and that life without this sort of examination is not worth living."[5] Eventually, the people of Athens had enough and gave Socrates a choice—stop with the philosophy or face the death penalty. If this seems like an awfully strict punishment, you might not realize just how obnoxious Socrates could be.

Facing death, he had this to say: "You are mistaken, my friend, if you think that a man who is worth anything ought to spend his time weighing up the prospects of life and death. He has only one thing to consider in performing any action; that is, whether he is acting justly or unjustly, like a good man or a bad one."[6] Socrates would say that Gob's worries about the next illusion, Lindsay's worries about finding a suitable partner in adultery, and Tobias's fears of being nude all fail to consider what is really important. Our crucial concern should always come down to one question: Am I being moral?

Socrates not only believed that self-reflection was essential—he thought it was *desirable*. Thinking critically and pursuing truth, he believed, leads to the greatest happiness. He often conveyed his teachings through stories, and one of his most famous is called the Myth of the Cave.[7] In this story, Socrates describes the human condition as analogous to people who are imprisoned—chained in a dark cave, where they never see anything real, but rather, only see shadows of real people and objects as they are reflected by firelight on the walls of the cave. As far as the prisoners know, the limited existence they experience in the cave is the whole of reality. If one of those prisoners were to get free and emerge from the cave into the light, he would be temporarily blinded, much like George Sr. probably was when he emerged from his underground hiding place. In the myth, though, things are even worse for those who see the light outside the cave. They're seeing it for the first time. After a period of adjustment, the escaped prisoners will finally see the world as it really is, rather than as shadowy reflections. They will, in fact, find that reality is far more fulfilling than cave life ever could be.

The story doesn't end there, however. If one of the freed prisoners were to return to the cave and explain to those still chained what he'd witnessed in the world above, they would laugh at him. They would scoff because, after being in the sunlight, his sight in the darkness of the cave would be far less keen than theirs. Like Buster Bluth, the freed prisoner would be inept in the everyday world of the cave dwellers. Unlike Buster Bluth, though, this ineptitude would be the result of seeing the truth. The former prisoner of the cave would claim to be happier than those chained below, but the cave dwellers would have no interest in leaving the warm complacency of cave life.[8]

What does this strange story mean? Socrates thinks that most of us spend our lives shrouded in illusion. We think we're great magicians, or awesome actors, or brilliant businessmen. Our understanding of the world is clouded and inaccurate, just like the people in the cave. Unlike the prisoners in the story, however, our chains are of our own making. We can break free anytime we like, just by opening our eyes, looking around, thinking critically, and refusing to let our minds be lulled and soothed by false but comforting beliefs. Shaking off our familiar misconceptions will be uncomfortable at first, just as it was uncomfortable for the prisoner when he first emerged into the light. But once we adjust to the sharpness and purity of reality, we'll achieve a happiness that is equally sharp and pure, and we'll never again be content to live a life of self-delusion. This is what Socrates called "happiness." Happy people are those who have seen illusion and reality and are in a position to choose between them. And every person in that situation will embrace truth, even when it's difficult or painful. Socrates says that this happiness is so compelling, he will not deviate from his pursuit of truth, no, ". . .not even if I have to die a hundred deaths."[9]

The Myth of the Cave shares some things in common with the pilot of *Arrested Development*. Think back to the first morning we met the Bluths. Michael was excited, because he believed he would be made partner that day. Michael was living in the cave with his family. He was not seeing reality for what it really was. Though he had worked at the company faithfully every day, he was totally unaware of what had been going on around him. He didn't know that everyone else in the family was happily living off the company money, that his twin sister had been in town for weeks, or that his father was in serious danger of being arrested for illegal business practices too numerous to mention. He dreamily reminds George Michael that family (not breakfast) is the most important thing.

George Sr.'s boat party was a turning point for Michael. It was then that Michael was yanked out of the warm, comforting darkness of the cave and shoved up into the cold light of reality. Within minutes, Michael's illusions about his father, his importance in the company, and his future were shattered. First he learns, publicly and with no explanation, that his mother, who as far as he knows doesn't even work for the company, bypassed him as partner. Moments later, he learns that his father has obviously been involved in some pretty bad stuff, as he is hauled away in handcuffs. Michael is shocked but quickly makes the decision to face reality. Now, he says, he really sees the world clearly. Now he knows the score. He will not return to the cave. He will go out and make a life for himself and his son in Phoenix, far away from his cave-dwelling relatives.

The remaining Bluths see things differently, however. From their vantage point in the cave, Michael looks like a fool. Where does he think he's going? In fact, Lucille "would rather be dead in California than alive in Arizona!" So, the family stages an intervention (which sounds more like an imposition). Michael, though, is already out of the cave. His eyes have adjusted to the sun, and he realizes that what he's done doesn't call for an intervention (I'd love to call it an imposition). Those in the cave and those who have emerged literally see things differently. Both prefer to remain where they are, and think those who do otherwise have made a huge mistake. This disagreement about how to live is clear throughout the series. Michael frequently criticizes his family's behavior, urging them to think about their lives and behave differently. Of course, this makes them angry and resentful (Lucille tells Michael that he is her second least favorite child, and Gob repeatedly calls him a robot . . . "the boy who couldn't cry"). Both sides think they're right, but Socrates's point is that only those who have emerged from the cave are in a position to make a call about which life is better. Socrates's claim is that a life of self-reflection and the critical search for truth is a better life, and will lead to more happiness. But let's take a look at the Bluths to see if the wisdom of Socrates can be confirmed.

Michael: "The Good One, the Moral One, the Fool."

Socrates would predict that Michael would be the happiest Bluth. After all, Michael is the member of the Bluth family who has most clearly emerged from the cave. He pokes his head back in sometimes to talk to his loved ones who still live there, and sometimes his perception of reality gets confused, but Michael tries to live a just, thoughtful life. He thinks critically about his actions and is aware of the fact that his behavior sometimes falls short of his own ideals. When this happens, he doesn't brush it aside, instead he reflects and considers how to behave better in the future. When Michael realizes that much of his dislike for Ann (George Michael's bland girlfriend) stems from jealousy over his son's affection, Michael takes steps to accept her as a part of his son's life.[10] Michael thinks this is the right thing to do, but he also sees this type of reflective life, of striving to know and better oneself, as the path to happiness. After getting to know Ann, however, Michael faces a sad truth—he really doesn't like her. Michael bravely faces the reality many parents face—he just doesn't like the person his son has chosen to date. Michael embraces the truth and is left disappointed.

The situation with Ann doesn't look like a fluke either. It looks as if Michael's level of happiness is proportionate to his level of self-deception. When is he saddest? When he sees reality most clearly; when Michael realizes that George Michael prefers to hang out with "Egg" over bikeriding with his dad. When he realizes (repeatedly) that his father doesn't trust him and continues to deceive him. When he's the only attendee at his mom's surprise party (twice). When he learns he is about to marry an MR F. When is Michael the happiest? When he is violating his own moral code by doing things he thinks he shouldn't. This usually involves sex with a forbidden partner—his brother's girlfriend, his son's teacher, his father's prosecutor. When he thinks his mother is genuinely concerned about his well-being after a car accident (really, she's framing him for an accident she caused; after all, she is one of the "world's worst drivers"). When he allows himself to be swept up in a delusion, like the time he almost married an MR F. Sure, he was unhappy when he discovered the truth, but Michael was happy as a clam as long as the deception held. Michael's awareness of reality makes him less happy than deception. Let's not be hasty though; perhaps some of the other Bluths can lend credence to Socrates's claim.

Gob: "They're Laughing with Me, Michael, They're Laughing with Me."

What do we know about Gob? He is in his mid- to late-thirties. He's never been in a serious relationship. He's been blackballed from the professional organization of his chosen trade (which he founded), the Magicians' Alliance. He has no stable income or home. Yet, Gob sees himself as a superstar. Despite the fact that his illusions end in failure more often than not, despite the fact that he can't find work and is considered a joke within his profession, and despite the fact that his family openly ridicules his trade, Gob sees himself as a master illusionist. His professional identity is tied up in a self-conception that has no basis in reality. There are many, many signs that would cue a normally functioning human being into the fact that Gob is a terrible magician. He regularly kills his live props (and then returns them from whence they came), his fireballs never trigger (but still, where did the lighter fluid come from?), and bystanders with no experience in magic can figure out how his illusions work. Yet Gob never sways in his deep, ungrounded belief that he is an excellent illusionist.

When he is made figurehead president of the Bluth Company (and we're fine with that), he immediately begins to self-identify as an expensive suit-wearing CEO (C'mon!), despite the fact that he does no real work for the company. And Gob's self-deception is not restricted to his professional life. He fancies himself a philanderer but rarely manages to actually "seal the deal." Just consider his marriage, which remained unconsummated for months, despite his repeated claims to the contrary. Gob has every reason to see his life as a failure. Yet he appears to be one of the happiest members of the Bluth family. He is confident and vivacious, certain he is always in the know, even though every adult member of his family repeatedly and successfully deceives him. In fact, the only times Gob appears to be unhappy are in the rare moments when he sees himself clearly for what he is (like when he wakes up in the hospital, having failed in an illusion and having been stabbed with a shiv. He made a huge mistake). But for times like that, Gob has a steady supply of forget-me-nows.

Lindsay: "You Call Yourself an Environmentalist, Why Don't You Go Club a Few Beavers?"

A stereotypical privileged daughter, Lindsay has not pursued a career. Instead, she devotes herself to maintaining her appearance and is a crusader for social justice. Unfortunately, Lindsay couldn't care less about any of the causes she spends her time championing. She wastes food at a benefit for world hunger,[11] opposes the war in Iraq because her hairdresser is being called to active duty (leaving her in need of a stylist), and is uncertain about what exactly she is supposed to be doing with the wetlands. "Dry them?" she guesses.[12]

Lindsay sees herself as a good mother, yet fails to recognize that her daughter is flunking out of school. Believing it to be an award, she has Maeby's expulsion letter from the "new age feel-goodery" Openings framed. She also considers herself to be a good daughter, but only visits her father in prison three times, with each visit motivated by the frustrated desire for leers and cat calls from the inmates (in her distorted version of reality, this would be the ultimate self-esteem boost). Lindsay brags about being employed while everyone else loafs around, but all she ever managed was a job *offer* (anyone can get a job offer), and she is fired for sleeping through the job after celebrating the job (offer) with money that she had not yet earned. To be fair, she did work at a clothing store once, but she was so invested in her public image she lied about the job, preferring that everyone believe she was stealing.

Similarly, Lindsay brags about keeping the house clean, but the two times she claimed to clean it she actually tricked someone else into doing the job (Lupe the first time, and Tobias—Mrs. Featherbottom—the second). Whenever she begins to see the ugly truth of her life, Lindsay immediately descends deeper within the cave. When she and Tobias finally admit to each other that their marriage is not working, she quickly switches gears. After an admittedly delusional suggestion of Tobias's ("it never works; these people somehow delude themselves into thinking that it might but—but it might work for us"), Lindsay proclaims their relationship an open marriage. She then happily engages in an imagined competition with Tobias over who will manage to have an affair first, even though neither of them do more than brag and scheme. Lindsay guards carefully against ever having to face her life for what it really is—and she's happy because of it.

Tobias: "You Blow Hard."

Tobias is perhaps the saddest member of the Bluth family, though he rarely recognizes this himself. He usually manages to glide along, deeply, happily self-deluded. Even more so than Gob, Tobias's professional identification is simply in his mind. Like Gob, Tobias has no reason to believe that he's any good at his chosen profession. After a few failed attempts to land work, Tobias is happy to spend most of his time on the couch. He blissfully wallows in his conception of himself as a misunderstood actor who strives for work, while actually watching bad TV and experimenting with his wife's wildly overpriced beauty products.

Tobias twists every situation to better match what he takes himself to be (an actor) and what he takes himself to be doing (searching for his breakthrough role). Despite good evidence to the contrary, Tobias insists on understanding his gym buddy, Frank, as anything but what he really is. When it becomes clear that Frank is not interested in him sexually, Tobias hears "agent" and assumes it to mean "talent agent." He misunderstands Frank as saying that he works for the CAA (Creative Arts Agency), when in fact he works for the CIA (Central Intelligence Agency). He interprets Frank's request that he be a mole as Frank wanting him to don a giant mole suit and act out a role.[13] Common sense tells us that we should understand ambiguous words in the most reasonable way, given the context, but Tobias's single-minded desire for the world to conform to his dreams leads him to contort his understanding of simple information in such a way that his own delusions are not threatened.

Tobias's sexual orientation is a running joke and a continuing mystery in the show. It isn't clear whether or not Tobias is gay because Tobias himself doesn't know. He's a tragic character, because it's clear that he does love his wife and daughter (this is undeniable when you remember that, after being kicked out of the house, he becomes Mrs. Featherbottom to spend more time with them).[14] The fact that outing himself would result in the end of his marriage is compounded by Tobias's deep sexual repression, of which his never-nude syndrome is one manifestation (it's exactly what it sounds like, and there are literally dozens of them). His level of repression suggests that Tobias would find having a sexual relationship with a man just as challenging as with his wife. We're also told that he and Lindsay do, on extremely rare occasions, manage to have enjoyable sex. So, while Tobias isn't clearly gay, he's certainly unaware of his own sexual nature.

Despite these extremely deep-rooted problems, Tobias has worked himself into such a high level of denial about his issues that he understands himself as actually being the person he would like to be. He proudly announces that he has sex with his wife (though her own level of sexual frustration tells us he doesn't), he proclaims himself a fabulous actor, and he thinks of himself as a loving father who has a strong relationship with his daughter (everything she does tells us that she looks on him with embarrassment and contempt). While maintaining his self-deception, Tobias seems relatively happy, most of the time. Strangely, however, at times he manages to have moments of clarity when he realizes his life is really nothing like the dream world he works so hard to keep going. When this happens he succumbs to overwhelming despair, alone, in his cutoffs, weeping in the shower.

Arrested Development follows the Bluths through several years of their lives, during which we watch Michael struggle for self-awareness yet find misery. We also watch the others maintain happiness in self-deception. So it looks like Socrates's prediction about self-awareness leading to happiness doesn't match up with the evidence. That means it's time to consider another philosopher.

The Arresting of Happiness

In *The Conquest of Happiness*, the philosopher Bertrand Russell (1872–1970) gives an account of the relation between happiness and self-knowledge that more clearly accords with *Arrested Development*. Russell saw the greatest cause of unhappiness as the desire for knowledge—obviously, this is bad news for us philosophers. Rather than appealing to a hypothetical example like Socrates's cave, Russell uses his own life as his primary example. From a young age, he was an unhappy person for two reasons. First, he desired something essentially unobtainable—absolute certainty about the issues he most cared about. The only way to end this type of suffering was for Russell to change his desires to something short of absolute certainty, which is obtainable. The second reason for his unhappiness was his "preoccupation with himself."[15] Russell, like most philosophers, spent a lot of time thinking about himself, just as Socrates urged. He reflected on his behavior (judging some actions moral and others immoral) and his beliefs (judging some justified and others unjustified). This constant search for self-knowledge left Russell feeling inadequate and prevented him from finding much happiness in life. In time, he learned to be indifferent (his word) to himself and his shortcomings, and he found himself happier. Russell went so far as to say that "interest in oneself, on the contrary, leads to no activity of a progressive kind."[16]

There are, according to Russell, three types of people who come to be unhappy through reflection: sinners, narcissists, and megalomaniacs. Sinners constantly find fault in themselves. No matter what a sinner wants, he'll see it as something he shouldn't want. As a result, he either does something he doesn't want to do or does what he wants and disapproves of himself.[17] George Michael fits this description. He's infatuated with his cousin Maeby, but he knows that society at large (except maybe the French . . . he likes the way they think), and his family in particular, would disapprove of any sexual relationship the two of them might form. Rather than admit his desires to his cousin, he enters into a relationship with a boring girl, Annabell (I call her that because she's shaped like a . . . she's the belle of the ball!), with whom he's got nothing in common. He spends a lot of time with her family praying (they are on Bethlehem time), which he hates, and he goes so far as to waste money on music just to burn at Ann's Christian (pause) music bonfire. All the while he longs to be with his cousin, and goes out of his way to impress her, only to feel ashamed. When he and Maeby finally act on their feelings, he gets to second base (stealing it like Pete Rose), but the cost is that he is filled with so much self-loathing he can't be in the same room with her. If George Michael would just admit to his taboo sexual desires (like his Gangee and Uncle Oscar), rather than suppressing them, he would probably be happier.

The narcissist is in many ways the opposite of the sinner. When a narcissist reflects on himself he sees his good qualities to the point of admiring himself. This leads to a desire to be admired by others, and when that doesn't happen, suffering ensues.[18] This seems to be the type of unhappiness that Michael suffers from. Just think of how many times Michael looks for recognition—from his father, sister, brother, son, employees, or girlfriends—that he is a good person. Even when he behaves badly, he wants to be seen as doing the bad thing in as good a way as he can (when he steals his brother's girlfriend or sleeps with his son's teacher). If Michael spent less time obsessing over his virtue and more time taking pleasure in the things he does, he would be better off. In other words, if Michael were more like Gob, or if he actually took the "stupid pills" that George Sr. often accused him of taking, he would be happier.

The last category of unhappy people is the megalomaniac. Russell says these people want to be powerful and feared in the way that a narcissist wants to be well-liked. But unhappiness results when these people recognize the great difference between the power they feel they deserve and the little they actually have.[19] A case might be made for Gob exemplifying this type of person, but we have a better *Arrested* example in George Sr.'s secretary and mistress Kitty (the whore). Secretaries outside of the academic setting are fairly powerless. Michael saw the position as so unimportant he allowed Tobias, Lindsay, and Starla (the model Gob gave a firm offer to) to do it. As a mistress, Kitty saw herself as more important to George Sr. than his wife, so she felt she was entitled to at least as much power as Lucille. Nobody else, including George Sr., saw things this way. Instead they saw her as crazy (she was). If Kitty just accepted her powerlessness like Buster (who is perfectly content to let others shepherd him around), she could find happiness.

Russell also thought that there are external circumstances that, regardless of self-knowledge, prevent a person from being happy. You need to have a reasonable income that allows for food, shelter, and health care before happiness is an option. Yet, even with these things, certain personal traumas can prevent any chance at happiness. Chief among these, according to Russell, are the death of a child and public disgrace. Russell would think George Sr. extraordinarily lucky that, after being arrested by the SEC, he was able to do (and have) the time of his life in prison.[20] While these observations might seem obvious, it's worth noting that Socrates didn't even see it as a possibility that external circumstances could affect happiness; he thought self-knowledge was necessary and sufficient for happiness.

This isn't to say that Russell thought there was no benefit to some reflection, or that we ought never to reflect (you should see all the stuff this guy wrote!). Rather, he thought that in moderation, reflection could lead to additional happiness. Russell, himself a "deliciously witty" man, put it this way, "Perhaps the simplest way to describe the difference between the two sorts of happiness is to say that one sort is open to any human being, and the other only to those who can read and write."[21] What he meant by this was that the more knowledge you have, the more you are able to understand and accomplish, and reaching your goals brings a type of happiness that is not available to those who don't have any goals.

There are many opportunities for happiness, and some of those opportunities are not available to those who don't reflect. Doing little tricks (illusions; tricks are what a whore does for money . . . or cocaine) can lead to happiness, but if that's all you can do, you may not be as happy as people who can do more. Learning more about the world and about yourself increases the number of places you can find pleasure. George Michael, for example, derives pleasure from getting As in class, a pleasure not open to Maeby.

Russell's lesson is that self-reflection is more likely to hurt than to help. However, for those who desire a certain amount of self-reflection, it's not necessarily something to be avoided. If Michael and George Michael can get it together and learn how to engage in a level of self-reflection that is not all-encompassing, they will have opportunities for happiness that are not available to their less-reflective family members. So, the unexamined life isn't a huge mistake, but a touch of examination might not be a bad thing.

NOTES

1. Episode 12.
2. Episode 14.
3. Episode 27.
4. Plato, *Apology*, p. 29e.
5. Plato, *Apology*, p. 38a.
6. Plato, *Apology*, p. 28b.
7. The story is probably Plato's, though he puts it in the mouth of Socrates.
8. Plato, *Republic VII*, pp. 514-518.
9. Plato, *Apology*, p. 30c.
10. Episode 26.
11. Episode 1.
12. Episode 5.
13. Episode 45.
14. Episode 36.
15. Bertrand Russell, *The Conquest of Happiness* (New York: W.W. Norton & Company, 1996), p. 18.
16. Ibid., p. 18.
17. Ibid., p. 19.
18. Ibid., p. 20.
19. Ibid., p. 21.
20. Ibid., p. 17.
21. Ibid., p. 113.

KISSING COUSINS

Incest, Naturalism, and the Yuck Factor

Deborah R. Barnbaum

George Michael thought that Maeby may be his cousin, which may be a problem. Or maybe not. Can moral philosophy help us figure it out all these maybes?

Maeby is George Michael's first cousin; George Michael is Michael's son, Lindsay is Maeby's mother, and Michael and Lindsay are brother and sister. At the end of Season 3, it's revealed that Lindsay was adopted, which means that Maeby may not be biologically related to George Michael. But then again, she may be, since Maeby's birth is cloaked in a bit of shadow (at least it is right now, as I'm writing). Maeby's grandmother, Lucille, referred to Maeby as having been "made in a cup," which doesn't eliminate the possibility that Maeby is George Michael's first cousin (in the naughty biological way). What it does tell us is that George Michael's and Maeby's relationship is a bit mysterious. The "high cost, low quality mini-mansion" might not be the only thing to come crashing down if George Michael and Maeby get together.

Throughout Seasons 1 and 2, George Michael believed that Maeby was family—the biological kind—and that he shouldn't be kissing her, or doing much of anything else with her. George Michael believes hooking up with his first cousin is morally wrong. It's incest, a big no-no (despite the fact that in previous centuries, cousins married all the time). But what makes incest morally wrong?

As we'll see, there are a couple of philosophical reasons for thinking that incest is morally wrong, but ultimately both are as flawed as an attempt to make millions selling the Cornballer.

The Argument from Naturalism

One argument against incest is that it is "unnatural." We'll call this The Argument from Naturalism. An *argument*, in the formal sense, has both premises and a conclusion. *Premises* are just those claims offered as evidence for a conclusion. A *conclusion* is what we infer from premises. There are two things to look for in an argument. First, we want to know if the conclusion logically follows from the premises (if it does, then the argument is valid). Second, we want to know if the premises are actually *true* (if the premises of a valid argument are true, we call the argument sound).

Here are some activities that might fall prey to The Argument from Naturalism: incest, riding a Segway, and Buster's love for "Mother." The Argument from Naturalism, applied to these three Bluthy things, looks something like this:

	The Segway	**Incest**	**Loving "Mother"**
Premise 1	Riding a Segway is unnatural.	Incest is unnatural.	Being totally devoted to Mother is unnatural.
Premise 2	If riding a Segway is unnatural, then it's wrong.	If incest is unnatural, then it's wrong.	If being totally devoted to Mother is unnatural, then it's wrong.
Conclusion	Therefore, riding a Segway is morally wrong.	Therefore, incest is morally wrong.	Therefore, being totally devoted to Mother is morally wrong.

In each case, the conclusion follows from the premises. So the argument is valid. But all of you cousin-lovers out there will be happy to know that validity isn't enough for a good argument. The premises need to be true as well.

The first premise is typically defended by pointing to examples in the world. Most people manage to walk if they need to traverse 20 yards at a time, the Segway is a manmade device, and incidentally, it makes Gob look like a complete goof every time he hops aboard to putter along only slightly faster than if he were walking. Gob's riding a Segway is clearly unnatural. In our first example, then, the first premise looks true.

But what of Buster's love for "Mother?" Most people—most normal people—don't live with their mothers into adulthood, don't have a fanatic devotion to them, and don't sublimate their desires by dating their mother's "best friend and chief social rival"—women with the same age, address, social status, and name as their own mothers. Buster's love for his mother is unnatural. Similarly, it might be argued that incest is unnatural. Perhaps, like the Segway, there is something that just looks odd about incestuous relationships. Perhaps there are few incestuous relationships in nature, and genetic disorders are more likely to be passed on if close relatives have biological children. (Of course, this is also true for folks over forty who decide to have children). These facts support the premise that incest is unnatural. (They might also show that having children over forty is unnatural.)

The second premise states that if something is unnatural, it's morally wrong. Why should we believe this? Defenders of the argument might point to the value of nature—its beauty, its harmony, its perfection. While humans have done a lot to mess up this planet (George Sr., we're talking to you!), those things that are "natural" are somehow unblemished. As such, the claim goes, if it's natural, then it's morally acceptable, and if it's "unnatural," then it's morally wrong.

If you want to object to this argument, you'll have a pretty easy go of things. Both the first and second premises have considerable flaws. Luckily, there is a lot to learn from examining the flaws in the argument. When considering the first premise, we need to ask what is meant by the term "unnatural." To understand what is unnatural, let's try to define what is natural (the opposite of natural will be our definition of unnatural). Among possible definitions of the term, we could list:

Definition 1: Something is natural if it is found in nature.

Definition 2: Something is natural if it is not altered by human beings.

Definition 3: Something is natural if it is typical, usual, or most common.

Incest is found in nature, so Definition 1 won't help the incest-hater claim that George Michael's hooking up with Maeby, in what seems to be an incestuous relationship, is unnatural. This is one of the greatest challenges confronting the defenders of the Argument from Naturalism who adhere to Definition 1: All it takes is one incestuous relationship found in nature to derail the argument. Edgar Allen Poe married his cousin, as did Jerry Lee Lewis (Goodness gracious, great balls of fire!). And of course, thousands of cousins have married in earlier centuries. Unless we deny that humans are a part of nature, it looks like our own history shows that incest *is* found in nature, and in lots of cases.

Those who adhere to Definition 1 might respond by saying, "It is true that there are examples of incest in nature, but those aren't really natural." If this is the response, though, the incest opponent is either equivocating (using two different senses of the term *natural*), or he is simply denying the evidence.

Those who adhere to Definition 1 must defend not only premise 1, but also premise 2. The claim "that which is found in nature is beautiful, harmonious, or perfect, and thus is moral" is not uniformly true—and not by a long shot. Birth defects, tsunamis, and seals with a taste for mammal blood are all found in nature. But we're hard-pressed to say that these things are beautiful, harmonious, or perfect, let alone moral.

Definition 2 says something is natural if it isn't altered by humans. Does that help defenders of the argument? George Michael's hooking up with Maeby is *an action that involves human beings*, so it doesn't make any sense to say that only actions unaltered by human beings are natural! George Michael and Maeby are human beings, after all—and natu-rally so. *All* of their interactions involve other human beings (namely, each other!). We certainly don't want to say that every time they interact they're behaving unnaturally. This would make every thing we do with other people unnatural and immoral—including reproduction in the old-fashioned way.

We live in an environment that has been altered by human beings, an environment replete with yachts, model homes, and Frozen Banana Stands. Given that we're immersed in an environment that has been altered by human beings, it's hard to distinguish actions that are "natural" and those that are "unnatural." Take, for example, Maeby's mysterious origin.

If she was "made in a cup" for $130,000, it's possible that she was conceived using in-vitro-fertilization (IVF). One IVF method would involve taking an egg from Lindsay, taking some sperm from Tobias, fertilizing the egg in a Petri dish, and then implanting that fertilized egg in Lindsay. Some people will argue that IVF is unnatural and thus morally wrong. But is it any more "unnatural" than birth control, perfume, deodorant, caesarian sections, ultrasounds, or antibiotics? All of these actions involve "alteration by human beings." Advocates of the Argument from Naturalism will be forced to claim that using antibiotics (or deodorant, perfume, and other things that make us smell fabulous) is morally wrong.

This leaves us with the third definition: Something is natural if it is most common, most typical. According to this definition, it's not that the unnatural is never found in nature—it's simply that the unnatural is unusual, it isn't the norm. And what isn't natural, according to premise 2, isn't morally right.

Those who object to the Argument from Naturalism don't have much to say in response to premise 1 if defenders of the argument adopt Definition 3. It's easily and empirically proven that some actions—kissing someone you believe to be your cousin, riding a Segway, fanatical devotion to your mother—aren't typical. But the perils of using Definition 3 emerge when premise 2 is analyzed. Let's have a look at this in our trusty old argument form.

1. Incest is not typical, usual, or most common.
2. If incest is not typical, usual, or most common, then incest is morally wrong.
3. Therefore, incest is morally wrong.

The big problem here is obvious: something can be both unusual and uncommon, and still be completely moral (or at least not immoral). If it were immoral to be unusual, then it would be immoral to have a high IQ, to be exceptionally generous, or to have your hand bitten off by a seal. Clearly, though, these things are not immoral. Likewise, it would be immoral for a Bluth to be caring, insightful, or compassionate. But actually, we think Michael is morally good to the extent that he manifests these traits.

People who use the Argument from Naturalism often engage in a philosophical sleight-of-hand (illusion!) known as the fallacy of equivocation. This is the fallacy committed when a single word or phrase is used with two different meanings in order to draw a false conclusion. Many jokes in *Arrested Development* rely on instances of the fallacy of equivocation (*The Man Inside Me*, anyone?). When someone uses "unnatural" to mean "atypical or unusual" or "not found in nature" and then switches the meaning in the middle of the argument to "morally wrong" that person commits the *fallacy of equivocation*.

The Scottish philosopher David Hume (1711–1776) offered a critique alternately called *Hume's Law*, *The Fact/Value Distinction*, or the *Is/Ought Distinction* that undermines the Argument from Naturalism. Any argument that moves from a claim that some fact *is* true in the world, to the claim that something *ought* to be true in the world, is philosophically questionable. You're reading this book. It doesn't follow that you *ought* to be. *Arrested Development* got canceled. It *definitely* doesn't follow that it should have been.

The upshot is that the Argument from Naturalism isn't a sound argument. Both premises suffer from problems (so the argument, though valid, is not sound). Is there another way to keep George Michael away from Maeby, given that the Argument from Naturalism doesn't work?

The Yuck Factor, and the Wisdom of Repugnance

Among human beings, there's almost a universal response to incest: *Eeww! Gross! Yuck!* Might this visceral response tell us something about what's morally right?

There's no formal argument behind this reasoning. But there is nonetheless something philosophically intriguing here. The philosopher A. J. Ayer (1910–1989) argued that moral claims don't actually mean what we think they mean. Ayer's position, called *emotivism*, is that moral claims simply express our emotional response to a particular action or state of affairs. Saying, "It is morally wrong for George Sr. to steal from his shareholders," is nothing more than an expression of disgust for George Sr.'s actions. There is no way to logically prove that stealing from shareholder is wrong; all we have is our emotional reaction.

The near-universal *Yuck!* response to incest may be an example of emotivism. George Michael and Maeby may not be on the edge of doing something that is morally wrong; it may be that hooking up while everyone believes them to be biologically related is merely the type of action that would result in a response of "Yuck!" But so what? "Yuck!" is not a philosophical argument; it doesn't prove a thing about morality. The emotivist tells us that moral claims are personal reports of deep admiration or disgust, nothing more.

Contrary to Ayer, Leon Kass offers a defense of the yuck factor as a means of telling us what is morally right and wrong, what he calls the *wisdom of repugnance*. Kass presented a lengthy and impassioned essay against human cloning in 1997 (when a sheep named Dolly was the first mammal to be cloned). One of Kass's objections is that we all recognize that some aspects of cloning humans are simply offensive or grotesque. Imagine women giving birth to offspring who are genetically *identical* to themselves (are they giving birth to themselves?), or giving birth to individuals genetically identical to their own mothers or fathers (can I be my mother's mother?), or parents attempting to create genetically identical children to "replace" those who have died. Kass considers what this visceral response might tell us:

Revulsion is not an argument; and some of yesterday's repugnanaces are today calmly accepted—though, one must add, not always for the better. In crucial cases, however, repugnance is the emotional expression of deep wisdom, beyond reason's power fully to articulate it. Can anyone really give an argument fully adequate to the horror which is father-daughter incest (even with consent), or having sex with animals, or mutilating a corpse, or eating human flesh, or even just (just!) raping or murdering another human being? Would anyone's failure to give full rational justification for his or her revulsion at these practices make that revulsion ethically suspect? Not at all. On the contrary, we are suspicious of those who think that they can rationalize away our horror, say, by trying to explain the enormity of incest with arguments only about the genetic risks of inbreeding.[1]

According to Kass, there is wisdom in repugnance. The fact that we find something deeply repugnant, gross, or yucky might be reason for us to pause, to consider the enormity of our action, and to recognize its moral wrongness. This isn't a formal argument, akin to the Argument from Naturalism. It is, however, a reason that George Michael and Maeby might think twice.

Let's think about the yuck factor and the wisdom of repugnance. Do they offer the moral guidance George Michael isn't getting? Probably not. But there is a more significant philosophical problem here. It has to do with the *kind* of normative evaluation that we undertake when we say that an action is morally wrong. Normative ethics is the study of what is morally right or wrong, good or bad. But there are many types of normative evaluations—evaluations of rightness and wrongness, goodness or badness—that aren't moral evaluations.

What George Sr. did in swindling shareholders wasn't just *morally* wrong—it was *legally* wrong. Legal evaluations are a different type of normative evaluation than moral evaluations. Remember, according to George Michael, marrying your cousin was "almost made legal . . . we had the signatures." Tobias's cutoffs are waaaay too short, which is wrong—but this isn't a *moral* evaluation. It's an *aesthetic* evaluation. Aesthetics is the philosophical study of art and the nature of beauty. When we are grossed out by Tobias's short shorts, we are making an aesthetic normative judgment.

Which brings us back to the yuck factor and the wisdom of repugnance. How are we to know that the yuckiness that we feel when confronted with an act of incest is a clue to a *moral* normative evaluation, rather than an *aesthetic* normative evaluation? Maybe it's a clue to yet another type of normative evaluation. This isn't a dismissal of the yuck factor or a denial that we find incest repugnant. But it is a call to question why we in fact believe the yuck factor indicates immorality. The sight of someone picking his nose is disturbing. So is Rudy Giuliani in a dress. Are we willing to say that *being* Paris Hilton is immoral or that picking your nose is immoral?

George Michael never seems to get a straight answer about anything. Philosophical arguments about whether he should hook up with Maeby—even if she is his cousin—aren't forthcoming, either. It may have been morally wrong for George Michael to hook up with Maeby when he thought she was his cousin, but the Argument from Naturalism, the yuck factor, and the wisdom of repugnance haven't cleared anything up. It's enough to make you want to go out and invest in the Cornballer after all.

NOTE

1. Leon R. Kass, "The Wisdom of Repugnance," reprinted in Bioethics: Principles, Issues, and Cases, ed. Lewis Vaughn, Oxford University Press (New York), 2010, p. 430.

FREUDIAN ARRESTED DEVELOPMENT

Tim Jung

Analysts and Therapists for the Bluths

The Bluths need psychoanalysis. Everything from Lucille's criticism to Maeby's compulsive lying is indicative of deeper psychological issues. Even the two "good" members of the family, Michael and George Michael, experience difficulty keeping it together when it comes to their family's often ridiculous or dangerous antics. But in spite of these serious character flaws, the Bluths still have a certain charm.

Why are the Bluths the way they are? What causes them to be so *irrational*? Why can't Tobias see that the title on his business cards ("Analrapist") is *something more* than a combination of analyst and therapist? Sigmund Freud (1856–1939) would claim that Tobias has *unconscious* ideas and urges that are making themselves known.

Use Your Allusion: Freud

The passions represent the irrational side of us that's beyond our control, and, in turn, that pushes or drives us to act or think in ways that we had not intended. Consider the episode "Meat the Veals," in which Ann's mother, that "sweet piece of Veal," is so overcome with passion that she demands that Michael take her to his secular world so that she may please him "secularly."

Although Freud claimed to avoid philosophy,[1] the German philosophers Arthur Schopenhauer (1788–1860) and Friedrich Nietzsche (1844–1900) clearly influenced Freud's views about the irrational side of human nature. Earlier philosophers like David Hume (1711–1776) placed an important emphasis on the passions and human thought. But Freud took it to a new level, dedicating his life to studying the irrational side of human nature through what he called *psychoanalysis*, the study of the *unconscious*.

Perhaps an Attic Shall I Seek—The Unconscious

Freud had two theories of how the mind was constructed. Freud's original idea, the topography, consisted of the *unconscious*, the *preconscious*, and the *conscious* levels of the mind. The *conscious* is that which is readily available to us—what we are aware of. The *unconscious*, therefore, is the part of us that we are *not* aware of. Ideas or urges that are unconscious may cause symptoms or erratic behaviors. Consider George Sr., in the episode "Sad Sack," hiding in the attic and howling like a wolf.

> **Tobias:** Jesus, it's the wolf! That is the wolf! The wolf is upstairs!
> **Michael:** Think it's just my son's *Peter and the Wolf* record.

For Michael, there's no question about what is actually going on in the attic. Tobias, however, is unaware of what is happening and misinterprets George Sr.'s howling. This is like an unconscious urge or thought coming to the fore of the conscious—the urge or thought is lost in translation. The attic, for Tobias, is the unconscious—for Tobias is completely unaware of the actual source of the howling.

Michael's response to Tobias exemplifies Freud's idea of *repression*. Michael, in his creative excuses ("Peter and the Wolf" or "the house is settling") are just like the *forces of repression* that oppose and resist unconscious ideas. These unconscious ideas are repressed because, for some reason, they are too traumatic or troublesome to become conscious. George Sr. hiding in the attic is certainly a troublesome idea, as he should be in prison—and so, as the purpose or essence of repression is to keep something from becoming known, Michael keeps his family unaware of George Sr.'s whereabouts.[2]

The *preconscious* is the accessible middle ground between the entirely accessible conscious level of the mind and the completely blocked-off unconscious level of the mind. It is much easier for preconscious thoughts to enter into consciousness than it is for the unconscious to enter into consciousness. The preconscious includes memories that we are not conscious of at the moment but that we can retrieve at any time. So if Lucille did not have too much to drink at last year's Motherboy celebration, the events of that day would be preconscious for her. Preconscious ideas and thoughts may also contain words that are residues from a failed repression. Therefore, the content of the preconscious is not fully repressed, while unconscious ideas and thoughts are completely unknown and repressed.[3]

The *preconscious* could be explained, again, through George Sr.'s presence in the attic. Except this time let's take George Sr.'s presence in the attic as being known only by George Michael in the episode "Good Grief!"

Michael: Well, I meant it. So no more secret trips up to the attic, right?

Narrator: George Michael didn't want to betray his grandfather, but it appeared that his father already knew the truth.

George Michael: I have Pop-Pop in the attic.

Michael: What? The mere fact that you call making love "Pop-Pop" tells me you're not ready.

The idea of hiding George Sr. in the attic was *latent*, or held back from consciousness in the realm of the preconscious. It only becomes fully conscious when Michael realizes that George Michael was *not* calling sex with Ann "Pop-Pop." He was actually referring to George Sr. This middle ground of Michael being told and yet not knowing that George Sr. was hiding in the attic is precisely where ideas of the preconscious lie. Ideas in the preconscious are neither fully known nor fully unknown, but they may eventually become known.

Freud's Company Model

Freud's second model, while influenced by the topographical model, is more familiar to casual readers of Freud. This second model was the *structural model*, which involved the *id*, the *ego*, and the *super-ego*. Freud uses the German words "Es," "Ich," and "Über-Ich," but English translations use their Latin equivalents—*id/Es* means "it," *ego/Ich* means "I," and *super-ego/ Über-Ich* means "Super I" or "Over I." The *id* dwells only in the realm of the unconscious, while the *ego* and *super-ego* are located both in the preconscious and the unconscious.

The id, located in the realm of the unconscious, is the "oldest" part of our mental agencies. It contains the instincts, or the *needs* that require satisfaction and that are the cause of *all* activity.[4] Because of the external world, not all instincts or *needs* can be met or fulfilled the way the id would prefer them to be. The ego functions as a diplomat between the external world and the id, deciding when, where, and if these satisfactions should be met.

Michael provides a good model for what the ego does if we think of the Bluth Company as an individual. When the company stock is unfrozen in "Whistler's Mother," every family member begins clamoring for fulfillment of their individual "needs." Gob needs a yacht, Lindsay needs a club membership, and Tobias needs (is?) the Queen Mary. Michael, playing the role of the ego, tries to regulate the needs of his family, who are playing the role of the id, by delaying the satisfaction of those needs.

And then there's the super-ego. The super-ego is just another burden for the ego. Freud explains that the super-ego is developed by the parents, who offer love and threaten punishments, which are "signs to the child as a loss of love."[5] George Michael's relationship to his father is a good example of what the super-ego (Michael) demands of the ego (George Michael). The demands of the super-ego limit the satisfaction of the ego. Take, for example, the exchange between George Michael and Michael in the episode "Motherboy XXX," where George Michael wishes to go to the Christian camp "The Promise Land" with Ann.

> **Michael:** It–It's not about school, pal. It's more about family. Your Uncle Buster's been very depressed lately, and you haven't visited him. Family first. Or did they not teach you that at the Promise Land?
> **George Michael:** I don't know. You won't let me go.

The *ego* is pulled in every direction, and must juggle demands from the *super-ego*, the *id*, and the external world. Freud explains, "An action by the ego is as it should be if it satisfies simultaneously the demands of the id, of the super-ego, and of reality—that is to say, if it is able to reconcile their demands with one another."[6]

Prove It: Baiting the Unconscious

Freud believed that *parapraxes*, or everyday errors, betray unconscious impulses. We all fall victim to *parapraxes* such as slips of the tongue, slips of the pen, bungled actions, and misreadings. You don't have to be crazy to have a *parapraxis* or two every once in a while, but they are exceedingly common in the Bluth family.[7] As Tobias, the *queen of parapraxes*, says, "I suppose that we all do expose our inner desires, don't we?"

There aren't enough pages in this book to catalog all of Tobias's homoerotic actions and statements. So let's focus on Tobias's gaff in the pilot episode: mistaking a group of flamboyantly dressed men for pirates. Freud would say that this was no coincidence—Tobias had unconsciously intended to spend time with homosexuals, though perhaps not necessarily to protest the local yacht club's discriminatory policies.

In *The Psychopathology of Everyday Life*, Freud tells the story of a man who, in wanting a day to himself, had to nevertheless pay a visit to someone that he would otherwise prefer not to see. After begrudgingly boarding the train to his destination, the man inadvertently transfers to the wrong train, and goes back to his home, where he would rather spend his time.[8]

Freud would no doubt say that Tobias has repressed homosexual urges ("No, I'm not gay, Lindsay . . . how many times . . . must we have this . . . "). Tobias, thinking he is dressing as a pirate when he is actually dressing in Lindsay's clothing, is one thing. Joining a group of homosexuals for a protest is another. Tobias, like the man who transferred to the wrong train, is satisfying an *unconscious* urge. Freud believes that when it comes to making errors, there are very few coincidences. We pretty much have to agree with him in the case of Tobias, who says questionable things like, "Oh, I can just taste those meaty leading man parts in my mouth!" so frequently that Michael even suggests that Tobias tape record an entire day's worth of dialogue, thinking that he "might be surprised by some of [his] phrasing!"

Shémale and Misreadings

Freud maintains that many misreadings are caused by the reader's expectation of what's coming next. Consider Freud's example of a man who had read Homer so much that he always read "Agamemnon" instead of the German word for "supposed," *angenommen*. This is precisely the reason why we read "Shemale" (SHE-Male) instead of "Shémale" (Shuh-MAL-ay) on Lindsay's T-shirt, and why we, the audience, experience a *parapraxis* of our own.

The T-shirt, a gift from Maeby, is read as "Shemale" (SHE-Male) by the viewers and by Maeby because of Lindsay's voice. Lindsay's voice was gravelly and manly throughout this episode ("Sad Sack") due to a night of excited drunken screaming at a single's bar. Regardless, Steve Holt (!) finds Lindsay attractive. Maeby, fearful of losing her crush to her mother, lies to Steve Holt (!), telling him that her mother is actually a man who thinks that he can pass as a woman. Believing the shirt to be a heartfelt gift, Lindsay is oblivious to the joke being played on her.

Michael, Marta, *Ann* Other Freudian Slips

A slip of the tongue—a Freudian slip—occurs when a person intends to say one thing but says something else that *sounds or seems* similar to the original intended word. Recall the exchange between Michael and Marta in the episode "Marta Complex."

> **Marta:** So you're saying there's no one that you're even interested in?
> **Michael:** There was somebody for a little while, but it was too much of a brother . . . bother.

"Brother" and "bother" sound similar and betray an embarrassing thought or desire. Michael, of course, was in love with Marta, but couldn't do anything about it without ignoring his mantra that "family comes first." But the slips didn't stop there. After the chants of "Speech! Speech! Speech!" (for no one in particular) at a family party, Michael gives in. He closes with an even more telling slip, "To Gob and Marta. To love and happiness. *I love you all, Marta.*"

In addition, Michael is always forgetting Ann's name (Her?). On one occasion, Michael calls Ann "Egg"—another example of a Freudian slip. What inspires this slip? Ann's eating habits. George Michael tells us all about it.

> **George Michael:** Oh, it's so cute. She sometimes takes a little pack of mayonnaise, and she'll squirt it in her mouth all over, and then she'll take an egg and kind of . . . Mmmm! She calls it a "mayonegg." [*concerned pause*] Are you okay?
> **Michael:** I don't feel so good.

Michael was decidedly not okay. Later in that same episode, "The One Where They Build a House," Michael inadvertently replaces Ann's name with "Egg" when George Michael asks about buying the diamond cream that Lindsay mentioned earlier in the episode ("A million ****ing diamonds!").

> **Michael:** George Michael, I'm sure that Egg is a very nice person. I just don't want you spending all your money getting her all glittered up for Easter.

Due to the disgust and nausea induced by Ann's "mayonegg," Ann and the snack were inextricably linked in Michael's mind. This caused Michael, who has trouble recalling Ann's name in the first place, to refer to her as "Egg"—a reference, hold the mayonnaise, to what made Michael ill earlier in the episode.

Motherboy, or the Oedipus Complex

Although parapraxes provide good evidence for the existence of the unconscious, a lot of what goes on in the unconscious is unknown to us. The Oedipus complex is one example.

Motherboy, while awkward, is nothing compared to Freud's Oedipus complex. Motherboy, of course, is what Lindsay calls the "I'm in love with my mother dance thing" and is the main event in the episode "Motherboy XXX." According to Freud, the Oedipus complex is very important in the development of a boy's psychology. The complex derives its name from the Greek tragic hero, Oedipus, who kills his father and marries his mother—though the true identity of both his parents were unknown to him at the time.

Freud believed that every boy experienced the Oedipus complex. Put simply, the Oedipus complex manifests itself as the resentment of the young boy towards his father, who disrupts the child's enjoyment of his mother's affection.[9] Because of this resentment, the boy wishes his father would disappear. But the father steps in and prohibits anything from happening. The child would like to take the mother for his wife, but the father poses a daunting threat. This causes the child to *repress* or turn away from the Oedipus complex. In other words, the complex is pushed into the realm of the *unconscious*. The frustration toward the father and the affection toward his mother remain unknown to the child, that is, unless we're talking about Buster Bluth—but we'll get to that in a moment.

Ernest Jones, Freud's official biographer, writes that a failed repression of the Oedipus complex might result in the boy being abnormally attached to his mother and therefore "unable to love any other woman."[10] Even if the boy could detach himself from the love for his mother, the weaning would always be incomplete and the boy would perpetually fall in love "only with women who in some way resemble the mother."[11] Buster's relationship with Lucille Two is a perfect example of this: Not only is Lucille Two around Lucille One's age, they also share the same name! Buster makes no bones about his relationship with Lucille Two in the episode "Marta Complex."

Buster: Our relationship doesn't work?
Lucille 2: No, not as long as you keep getting me all mixed up with your mother.
Buster: It is exactly the opposite. I'm leaving my mother for you. You're replacing my mother.

George Sr. even needs to remind Buster of the father's prohibition in the episode "Justice Is Blind." Hours before his arrest, he says to Buster:

George Sr: No, no, no. Let me help you with that, son. Enjoy yourself tonight. Because you are out of here. I'm not going to spend my retirement watching you wipe your nose on your sleeve.
Buster: I can't breathe, Dad.
George Sr: (Gritting his teeth) Neither can I!!

From Buster's Motherboy mission "Operation Hot Mother" to calling his sister his new mother ("And is it just me, or is she looking hotter, too?"), most of Buster's behavior exemplifies his failed repression of the Oedipus complex. Take, for instance, his picture with Lucille in the *Balboa Bay Window* magazine in the "Marta Complex" episode. Included in the magazine is an article written by a young Buster, titled "Why I Want to Marry My Mother." This same article causes Stan Sitwell to comment later in the episode, "You know, it could be worse. He could want to marry your mother. (*Laughs.*) Oh, I'm sorry. Is your family not laughing at that yet?"

Totem . . . : Boyfights

Looking for the origin of the totem animal, an object of worship that watches over the tribe or clan, Freud examined primitive culture using psychoanalysis in his book *Totem and Taboo*. Charles Darwin (1809–1882) inspired Freud's answer: *the primal horde*. Darwin proposed that at one point, humanity was similar to bands of gorillas. One older male would live among many females and would drive out the younger males, much like the prohibitive father in the Oedipus complex. According to Darwin, this would prevent "interbreeding within the limits of the same family."[12] According to Freud, this angered the young males—so they devised a plot to unite and eat the tyrannical father after killing him. Sounds little like the sibling rivalry on *Arrested Development*. The plot of the episode "Making a Stand" echoes the unification of the brothers against the tyrannical father. Of course, instead of killing and eating George Sr., Gob and Michael hire J. Walter Weatherman (George Sr.'s one armed "scare-toy") to teach George Sr. a "lesson" about pitting them against each other.

According to Freud, with the obstacle to sexual desires gone, the brothers become divided. Such desires do not unite men—they divide men.[13] Each of the brothers wished to possess all of the females, as the murdered tyrannical father once did. Think of Marta from the "Marta Complex" episode—Gob, Michael, and even Buster ("Will somebody please punch me in the face?") fight over Marta. Sexual desires certainly do *not* unite men, as George Michael shows us in the series finale by punching Gob in the face for dating Ann (Her?).

According to Freud, because of this division, the brothers could afford no alternative but to renounce the women they all desired, the women who drove them to the murder of the tyrannical father in the first place. The totem animal—the sacred animal of the tribe—is a replacement of the lost father. The tribe worships the totem animal by murdering, consuming, and subsequently mourning it. But even within the ritual there is an attempt at self-justification: "If our father had treated us in the way the totem does, we should never have felt tempted to kill him."[14]

. . . and Taboo: Les Cousins Dangereux

Freud also wrote about incest outside of the Oedipus complex in the book *Totem and Taboo*. The primal brothers become divided after murdering their tyrannical father, and so the taboo of incest was meant as a remedy that would keep them from fighting over women in their own tribe. Whatever its true origin, the prohibition against incest remains with us. For example, if you were to sing a karaoke rendition of "Afternoon Delight" with a relative—say, your niece or nephew—you might get some strange looks.

George Michael is concerned with the prohibition of incest to the point of asking if kissing Maeby is illegal in the pilot episode. Strangely enough, each time they break the taboo, George Michael and Maeby return to the prohibition against incest. After kissing Maeby, in the first episode, George Michael yells, "I knew it was against the law!" when the SEC shows up.

In the episode "The Righteous Brothers," George Michael kisses Maeby and "steals second." Their fun is ruined, however, when Gob walks in and says, "Dad's gonna be crushed!" referring to George Sr., who he hid in the crawlspace beneath the collapsing model home. George Michael, panicking, responds, "We don't have to tell him!" thinking that Gob was talking about Michael.

Gob has a similar reaction to the idea that he has transgressed the prohibition of incest. In the episode, "Family Ties," Michael is investigating Nellie—NOT Tobias—and discovers three things: (1) Nellie is possibly his sister, (2) Nellie is a prostitute, and (3) Gob/Franklin is her pimp. Gob offers Michael a "family discount" for her services. Michael responds, "Family discount is right, Gob. This is the sister that I've been talking about." Gob responds tearfully, "Maybe I should have been getting a family rate. Oh my God."

Pop-Pop Gets Put on the Couch?

Who knows in what direction Freud's theories might have gone if he had met the Bluths during the development of psychoanalysis? Tobias's latent homosexuality, Buster's Oedipus complex, and even Michael's need to keep his family together would have made excellent case studies. And we will just have to wonder what Freud would have made of Tobias, the never-nude.

NOTES

1. Sigmund Freud, "An Autobiographical Study," *The Freud Reader*, ed. Peter Gay (New York: W. W. Norton & Company, 1995), p. 37.

2. Ibid. "Repression," p. 105.

3. Ibid. "Ego and the Id," p. 632.

4. Sigmund Freud, "Instincts and Their Vicissitudes," *General Psychological Theory*. Introduction by Philip Rieff (New York: Touchstone, 1997), p. 85. Sigmund Freud, *Outline of Psycho-Analysis* (New York: W. W. Norton & Company, 1989), p. 14.

5. Ibid., p. 77.

6. *An Outline of Psycho-Analysis*, p. 15.

7. Sigmund Freud, *New Introductory Lectures on Psychoanalysis*, ed. James Strachey (New York: W. W. Norton, 1990), p. 29.

8. Sigmund Freud, *Psychopathology of Everyday Life*, ed. James Strachey (New York: W. W. Norton, 1990), p. 290.

9. Ernest Jones, *Hamlet and Oedipus* (New York: W. W. Norton & Company, 1976), p. 75.

10. Ibid., p. 77.

11. Ibid., p. 77.

12. Sigmund Freud, *Totem and Taboo*, ed. James Strachey (New York: W. W. Norton, 1990), p. 156.

13. Ibid., p. 178.

14. Ibid., p. 179.

and: the-op.com

DON'T KNOW THYSELF

Gob and the Wisdom of Bad Faith

Daniel P. Malloy

Socrates once said, with his life on the line, "The unexamined life is not worth living."[1] But he never looked at the results of that examination. (His fellow citizens executed him.) So what if someone examined his life, and found it not worth living? In that case, it would be better to avoid the examination in the first place. In fact, that's just the way that Gob Bluth lives his life, and we should respect him for it.

In "S.O.B.s," Gob pretends to be a waiter, only to find himself really being a waiter. This scene reminds me of Jean-Paul Sartre's well-known example of the waiter in the café, the one who is just a bit too much like a waiter—too eager, too concerned, too perfectly waitery. As Sartre describes him,

His movement is quick and forward, a little too precise, a little too rapid. He comes toward the patrons with a step a little too quick. He bends forward a little too eagerly; his voice, his eyes express an interest a little too solicitous for the order of the customer.[2]

Sartre gives this example to illustrate his concept of *bad faith*. But, as we shall see, Gob's initial act in "S.O.B.s" is not an act of bad faith. It is only later, when Gob really decides that he is a waiter that he enters into bad faith.

Gob, in fact, lives large parts of his life in bad faith. He tells himself that he is a great magician, that he can run the Bluth Company, that he loves Marta, and that everyone loves him, and he acts according to those beliefs. Each of these acts, among many others, is an instance of bad faith. Gob tries constantly to fill various roles for which he is simply unsuited.

Gob isn't alone in bad faith, however. The rest of the Bluth clan keep him company on occasion. But outside of a few isolated incidents, such as when Buster bashes his mother in order to fit in with his siblings ("Bringing Up Buster"), the Bluths are largely too self-involved to be in bad faith. The only exception (aside from Gob, of course) is Michael, who we discover in the final season is living in bad faith about precisely how self-involved he is ("The Ocean Walker"). Gob is unique, a perfect case study of bad faith. Most people occasionally enter into bad faith, but Gob lives there—and good thing, too!

Gob is wiser for it. Not only does Gob's bad faith make him happier, it also makes him a better person. For Gob, the ancient wisdom must be altered: *Don't* know thyself, Gob.

Gob Isn't Just Deceiving Himself

In *Being and Nothingness*, Sartre reluctantly identifies bad faith and self-deception. He says, "We shall willingly grant that bad faith is a lie to oneself, on condition that we distinguish the lie to oneself from lying in general."[3] There is good reason for his reluctance—when we think a bit, we can see that self-deception and bad faith are two distinct concepts. As tempted as we may be to accuse Gob (or any other Bluth) of self-deception, such an accusation wouldn't be correct. Gob lives in bad faith, but no one can live in self-deception.

So, what makes self-deception impossible? After all, it's fairly common to say that so-and-so is just deceiving himself. But common and correct aren't the same thing. Don't deceive yourself about deception: if the person being deceived already knows the truth, then the deception has no chance of succeeding. When Buster deceives Gob into believing that George Sr. is controlling Larry (George's surrogate while he is under house arrest), the entire act is based on Gob not knowing the truth about who is actually controlling Larry ("Mr. F"). Had Gob realized that Buster was giving Larry his orders, he would never have been fooled. In the case of so-called self-deception, a single person would have to know the truth of the matter (in order to deceive) and not know it (in order to be deceived). Hence, self-deception isn't possible.

So, if bad faith is possible, we must distinguish it from self-deception more clearly than Sartre did. This can be done fairly easily.[4] Bad faith is existential; self-deception is epistemic. That means that while self-deception is about belief and knowledge, bad faith is about living and acting. It is not necessary to *believe* anything to be in bad faith. For Gob, living in bad faith means that he is acting like something he isn't. It's more like pretending than it is deception. But the pretense of bad faith should be distinguished from other forms of pretense. Occasionally, an actor or actress will be praised for "disappearing" into his or her part—making the audience forget that this is a person playing a part. The person living in bad faith tries to do the same—disappear into a role. Only, in this case, Gob's audience is himself.

Let's dive a little deeper. For Sartre, there are two kinds of things in the world: beings-in-themselves (*en-soi*) and beings-for-themselves (*pour-soi*). Beings-in-themselves simply are what they are. They are defined by other beings, often before they even exist. For instance, a carpenter builds a table. Before he begins to build, he defines his project. He chooses the materials, designs the table, and establishes what his finished product will be and what it will be used for. Before it comes into existence, the table has its essence assigned to it. The carpenter is a being-for-itself. Unlike the table, the carpenter doesn't have a pre-given essence. He chooses to become a carpenter, just as he chose to build a table. Humans are beings-for-themselves, and as such we are free beings. Unlike a table, a human can choose to be this or that. When we try to deny this fact, this freedom, we enter into the realm of bad faith. Bad faith consists in acting as though one was not free, as though one was a being-in-itself. As Sartre says, "The waiter in the café cannot be immediately a café waiter in the sense that this inkwell *is* an inkwell, or the glass is a glass."[5]

Although most of the Bluths lie to themselves, or try to, Gob is uniquely suited to guide our discussion of bad faith. Gob is sometimes like most of the rest of the Bluths—selfish, narcissistic, vain, and worse—but he is also often driven by a need to be thought well of by others. His quests for his father's approval and Michael's respect, for acceptance by the world at large, for love and self-respect, all lead Gob to deny his freedom, to disappear into parts, to live in bad faith.

Gob Plays His Roles

Michael also engages in bad faith. At least in the final season, much of Michael's motivation is wrapped up in how he's viewed by others. It's not so much that he *is* a good person, as that he needs to be *seen as* a good person. He, like Gob, is playing a part. Michael plays the part of the good one, the selfless one, the reliable one, "the living saint," the put-upon member of the Bluth family. Michael's acts of bad faith do not form the core of his existence, though. In this, Gob is unique. He is so bound to his bad faith that his life would be shattered without it.

Just consider Gob's various careers. He began the show as a magician (illusionist!), moved on to being the titular president of the Bluth Company, and then became a ventriloquist—taking temporary gigs along the way as a waiter, a pimp, and an executive at a rival development company. Gob isn't especially good at any of these jobs; for some he has no qualifications at all, and he knows it. But he desperately wants to be good at all of them. In each career, he tries to fill the role to a T. As a magician (illusionist!), he founded the Magician's Alliance—only to be blacklisted by them ("Pilot"). As president of the Bluth Company, he tried hard to imitate his father—wearing George Sr.'s suit and firing everyone ("Afternoon Delight"). In each case, Gob behaves in the way he thinks he ought to, rather than recognizing and accepting that he is making free choices.

Sadly, Gob's bad faith isn't limited to his "professional" life. It also plagues his romantic relationships and encounters. In particular, it was ever present in his relationship with Marta. Recall his hasty decision to make up with her. The instant she accepts, Gob realizes that he's "made a huge mistake" ("Key Decisions"). What was his mistake? From Sartre's perspective, Gob's mistake was that he denied his freedom, but not in the same way that anyone who enters a relationship denies his freedom. Gob denied his freedom by treating himself as "any man." Convinced by Michael that any man would be lucky to have Marta, Gob acts as "any man" should. The trouble is that Gob isn't "any man." No one is. Gob is an individual, and as such does not fit into the mold of "any man." In getting back together with Marta, he denied that fact about himself.

Gob's brush with matrimony is likewise rife with bad faith. We can see this in two aspects of his marriage to the "Bride of Gob," played by Amy Poehler (the character, although appearing in several episodes, is never named other than Gob's misguided attempt to remember her name, when prompted by Michael). First, there's Gob's continuing insistence that the marriage was consummated, in spite of his inability to remember the event. Then there's the fact that Gob briefly slips into the role of the ideal husband, or at least of the long-suffering husband.

One of Gob's previous romantic encounters led to another instance of bad faith. We are not told much about his relationship with Eve Holt beyond the fact that it resulted in Steve Holt (!). Gob's relation to Steve involves bad faith in two ways. First, there are Gob's various attempts to deny that Steve is, in fact, his son. In a confrontation with Michael, Gob even denies the validity of DNA tests:

> **Gob**: Hey, can you do me a favor? A young neighborhood tough by the name of Steve Holt will be dropping by, and . . .
> **Michael:** Your son?
> **Gob**: According to him.
> **Michael:** And a DNA test.
> **Gob**: I hear the jury's still out on science. ["Notapusy"]

Accepting one's freedom also means accepting the consequences of one's choices. Gob goes to extremes to deny this particular consequence, however. At one point he goes so far as to dose himself with a Forget-Me-Now ("Forget-Me-Now").

On the other hand, when Gob does acknowledge Steve as his son, he goes to the other extreme, once again trying to play a role for which he's unsuited. Like many parents, Gob decides he won't make the same mistakes his parents did. So, instead of mimicking the absentee parenting of his father, Gob attempts to mimic the parenting style of Ward Cleaver. For instance, in

"Making a Stand" Gob opens a banana stand with the help of Steve Holt (!). By including Steve, he's trying to avoid being the neglectful father that George Sr. was. The trouble is that Gob isn't Ward Cleaver. He's an adult in name only.

The examples we've considered so far all seem to point to the conclusion that bad faith is, well, bad. But if we look at some of the times when Gob is happiest, or making others happiest, he's living in bad faith then as well. The example that springs to mind is when Gob plays catch with his father in the prison yard. Gob knows full well that he is not that kind of son, nor is George Sr. that kind of father. Nevertheless, they both have their fun—until Gob gets stabbed by White Power Bill ("Key Decisions").

Be Yourself, Gob

Although bad faith generally seems to work out for Gob, there's a reason Sartre labels it "bad" faith. Gob seems happiest when living a lie, but his happiness doesn't make the lie any more honest. Further, given the number of bad faith scenarios we've outlined, it would seem difficult *not* to live in bad faith. Indeed, it is. Sartre acknowledges as much. He says, "If bad faith is possible, it is because it is an immediate, permanent threat to every project of the human being."[6] In everything we do, there is always the risk of bad faith. It is a constant temptation to simply play our role in life. Consciously trying not to be in bad faith can itself be a form of bad faith. Sartre calls this form of bad faith "sincerity." If we tell Gob that instead of living in bad faith he should be sincere or just be himself, Sartre will laugh at us in a mocking, French way.

Recall the definition of bad faith: treating a thing that is for-itself as a thing that is in-itself. By Sartre's understanding, any demand for sincerity does just this. He even says, "The essential structure of sincerity does not differ from that of bad faith."[7] When we ask Gob to be sincere, we are not asking him to accept his essential and radical freedom, or his responsibility for the events in his life. Instead, we are acting as though there's some other independent essence of Gob—his Gobness, we might say, just as there's an essence of being a chair (it's "chairness"). In demanding sincerity, we want Gob to act in conformity with his Gobness, to play the role of Gob as we've come to know and tolerate him. This involves denying his freedom just as much as any other form of bad faith. Just because Gob is playing the role of Gob doesn't mean that he isn't playing a role.

Since sincerity itself is just another form of bad faith, we seem to be left with few, if any, options. We are doomed to lives of bad faith, and we might as well get used to them. All is not so bleak, however. The term *bad faith* already points the way to the alternative: *good faith*. So what is good faith? How is it distinguished from sincerity? And what happens when someone lives in good faith? Remember, the problem with sincerity boils down to treating someone as something that he or she is *not*. For Gob to be "sincere," he must treat himself as though he had no choice but to act in this way. But the facts are otherwise. Gob is a radically free being. Whatever he is doing at the moment, be it an illusion or talking to his brother or having sex with his former high school civics teacher, he chose to do it—and he can choose to quit.

Good faith, then, is not "being oneself" but accepting the type of being one is, accepting radical freedom and responsibility (the two go together). It's a frightening prospect: to live without identifying with one's roles, without guidelines telling one how to live. It is a goal that is rarely achieved because it is difficult to break out of our roles, or even to be sure that we have. Oddly enough, one of the few times that we certainly act in good faith is when we act ironically. For instance, Gob is acting in good faith when he pretends to be waiter. He knows he's not a waiter. He's just Gob, choosing to have a laugh at the idea that he'd work for a living.

The terms *good faith* and *bad faith* already imply which we ought to prefer. Sartre is an advocate of life lived in good faith. But what do we gain by good faith? Self-respect, dignity, maybe—not much, really. We do, however, lose quite a bit. We lose our roles, our guidelines—indeed, even our identities. What we get in return is little compensation. We get something we already had: freedom, freedom without limits. Sartre openly acknowledges that this isn't a great deal. We're taught to value freedom, but absolute freedom like this is paralyzing at best. As Sartre puts it, "Man is condemned to be free."[8] The only difference good faith makes is that we acknowledge it.

Gob Makes Huge Mistakes in Good Faith

According to Sartre, good faith is a struggle. On one hand, we easily fall prey to bad faith because it's comforting to have roles to play. Good faith, on the other hand, is frightening and difficult for most people. In some ways, Gob seems to be an exception to this rule. He often goes from bad faith to good, and back again—sometimes in the course of a single scene. Gob seems to slip easily into good faith, but has trouble maintaining it. The siren call of bad faith is just too strong. Nonetheless, let's take a closer look at some instances of Gob's good faith, and see what the outcome is.

Our first example of Gob's good faith is, appropriately, a parody of Sartre's most famous example of bad faith. When Gob becomes a waiter in "S.O.B.s" he does so in good faith. At first, he is not mistaking himself for a waiter—he is play-acting, in an ironic way, at being a waiter. He's making a joke. Because of the distance that he acknowledges between himself and the role of "waiter," it's obvious that Gob took on the mannerisms freely. He didn't initially deny his freedom in playing this role. It's only later, when Gob starts believing that he really *is* a waiter that he acts in bad faith. When he flirts with his wealthy customers and gets angry with Lindsay for messing up the dinner, Gob has slipped back into bad faith.

Such is the temptation and danger of roles. They lead us very easily to identify ourselves with them and deny that we have chosen to occupy them. There is one role, however, that Gob occupies often, but that rarely leads him to bad faith. This is the role of the bum or the mooch. Many bums and mooches like to make excuses for their status, thereby denying the element of choice that led them to be bums. Gob, to his credit, does not. He is quite honest with himself at least, about why he's a bum: he doesn't like to work. Again, in "S.O.B.s," the whole point of Gob's little joke is the laughable idea that Gob should get a job. One may not respect the lifestyle, but there's something to be said for the honesty. That honesty is limited however. Gob's choice to be a bum often leads to dishonesty toward others, as when he seduces his father's secretary, Kitty, so that Michael will keep supporting him ("Visiting Ours"), or any of the many times he lies to Michael.

The most common and poignant temptation that leads Gob to bad faith is his need for acceptance and approval. This may be the case for most of us, but it is especially true for Gob. His mother is distant, his father is disappointed, his siblings don't take him seriously—you get the idea. But occasionally it is Gob's striving for acceptance that leads to good faith—mainly when that striving fails and Gob realizes he is unloved for a reason. It sounds cruel, but there is a reason Gob remains unloved: he's a narcissistic boob. As he tells Buster, "I'm the pathetic one, Buster, not you. I totally freaked out in front of that prosecutor today. Like a little girl. In a little dress. Little saddle shoes. Little pigtails" ("Sad Sack"). Realizing that he's chosen to be a narcissistic boob is Gob's ultimate act of good faith.

So, should we strive to live in good faith? That's too general. Some of us surely should. But should Gob? Look at what he gets from good faith: bad faith, deceiving others, and soul-crushing revelations. That doesn't sound like a great deal.

The Wisdom of Bad Faith

The intuition we have about the wrongness of bad faith is actually, according to Sartre, based on a faulty ontology. We believe that people shouldn't have to pretend, shouldn't have to deny who they truly are. People should accept themselves as they are and be happy with that. The trouble is that, according to Sartre, who we "truly are" is nothing more than freedom. For Gob to be who he truly is at each moment means nothing more than to choose at each moment. One moment he may choose good faith, and accept that each of his actions and all of their outcomes are the result of his choices, and the next moment he may choose bad faith, and believe that his actions are dictated by the role he plays or the social position he occupies. So, why choose one over the other?

We often choose one thing over the other because one will make us happier than the other. This explains a number of the choices we make, from chocolate instead of vanilla to going to college instead of going to jail. It may also point us in the right direction for Gob. When is Gob happiest? If we're honest, we'll have to say that he seems happiest when he's living in bad faith. It's easy to see why: Playing a role provides a degree of security and reassurance. For someone as fundamentally directionless as Gob, good faith must be a paralyzing experience. Gob has been called many things, most of them unflattering, but never responsible. Good faith must be a nightmare for Gob. Bad faith, on the other hand, is a fluffy down comforter. It keeps Gob safe and warm. It's debatable whether the happiness involved in bad faith is genuine happiness, but the fact is that it seems to satisfy Gob.

Sometimes, though, we forgo our own happiness in favor of the happiness of others. Admittedly, Gob rarely does this (in his defense, though, nor do any of the other Bluths except for Michael and George Michael). Nonetheless, his actions do make other people happy or unhappy, even if he doesn't intend them to. So, when are the people in Gob's life happy? When

Gob lives in bad faith, Steve Holt (!) gets a good father, Michael gets a caring brother, Buster gets a protector, and the whole world gets a clown. This shouldn't be surprising. After all, what most often leads Gob into bad faith is his desire for approval, so it's only natural that he is more likable when he plays a role. When he lives in good faith, on the other hand, Gob tends to be a selfish mooch and a loser. He brings people down.

If what I've said so far is true, that Gob and the people around him are all better off when he lives in bad faith, why shouldn't he just go ahead and live in bad faith? For Sartre, he's denying his freedom. I have two responses to Sartre. First, so what? What's so important about embracing radical freedom, especially if it makes Gob miserable? Second, isn't it possible to freely choose bad faith?

Socrates advised us to know ourselves, because the unexamined life is not worth living. Gob shows us the danger of knowing ourselves and examining our lives. Gob is the sage of bad faith. He has shown us the way. Reject authenticity! Embrace a role or two! Twenty! As many as you want! As many as you can! That way lies security and happiness; the other way, insecurity and madness!

NOTES

1. Plato, *Apology*, trans. Harold North Fowler (Cambridge: Harvard University Press, 1971), p. 133.

2. Jean-Paul Sartre, *Being and Nothingness*, trans. Hazel E. Barnes (New York: Washington Square Press, 1984), p. 101.

3. Ibid., 87.

4. This distinction is further explored and elaborated in Herbert Fingarette, *Self-Deception* (London: Routledge & Kegan Paul, 1972). What follows is an unorthodox interpretation of Sartre.

5. Sartre, 102.

6. Ibid., 116.

7. Ibid., 109.

8. Jean-Paul Sartre, "The Humanism of Existentialism," *Essays in Existentialism*, ed. Wade Baskin (New York: Citadel Press, 1993) 41.

PART TWO

A BUSINESS MODEL

DR. FÜNKE'S 100 PERCENT NATURAL GOOD-TIME ALIENATION SOLUTION

Jeff Ewing

The Bluths are just like your family, at least if your father, the former president of a company, went to prison due to a number of shady activities. And if all your family members are crazy (in the therapy-or-felony way, not in the normal cute-dysfunctional family way). And if there is some strange, semi-incestuous dynamic going on between . . . most of you. On second thought, the Bluths are nothing like most American families, but still, like most American families, the Bluths are alienated by the capitalist system. Uncle Karl (Marx) will help us sort this out.

Happy Bluthday to You! The Bluth Family History

George Bluth Sr. was the CEO of the Bluth Company, which builds mini-mansions, among other activities (including owning and operating a frozen banana stand). The Bluth children, wealthy and accustomed to getting whatever they want, don't really work for a living. They coast on Daddy's money. As George Bluth Sr. says, "There's always money in the banana stand" (and he means it literally).

Things take a turn for the worse, though, when George Sr. is arrested by the SEC (Securities and Exchange Commission, for those of you who want to know) for defrauding investors and spending company money as though it were the Bluth's personal bank account. This is where *Arrested Development* begins, with the Bluth Company, fortune, and family in shambles. Michael, the normal one, takes on the responsibility of keeping the family together, getting his dad out of jail, and saving the Bluth Company. Unfortunately, standing in the way of these goals are the rest of the Bluths. As we'll see, the personal flaws of the Bluths are manifestations of *alienation*, which results from the capitalist system they perpetuate.

Marx and Alienation—Or, How to Never Succeed in Life While Really, Really Trying

According to Karl Marx (1818–1883), the main problem with capitalism, and the reason we need to move from capitalism to socialism (and later, to philosophical communism) is not that capitalism makes people poor. To be sure, Marx did believe that capitalism makes people poor. In fact, it makes people rich *through making other people poor*. The way to become rich is to get people to work for you (as a capitalist) for as little as possible, while making you as much money as possible—a process that can only result in the increased relative and absolute poverty of workers. The primary Marxian problem with capitalism is that capitalism involves some individuals controlling others, and the control is always for the benefit of the powerful capitalist rather than the good of the powerless laborer.

Marx argued that as surely as economic systems had inherent guiding laws and defining characteristics, so do species have distinct traits and forms of activity. These traits and forms of activity constitute a species' essence. And, Marx says, "Free conscious activity constitutes the species character of man."[1] No other species chooses its activity. On one hand, the activity of animals is automatic, a product of instinct. Humans, on the other hand, including Buster Bluth, are capable of choosing their own activity, and thus have control over their own lives. The human essence (or, as Marx frequently calls it, "species-being") is the ability to choose freely one's own life activity. This activity is expressed through production, through people (even Gob) creating in a way that manifests their vision of how the world should be, and in response to the true needs of others.

The bad news, as Uncle Karl (Marx) sees it, is that capitalism alienates people from their ability for free conscious activity. By definition, one thing is alienated from another thing when the two belong together, but something else separates them. Capitalism, Marx argues, alienates workers in four primary ways. First, the workers are alienated from the actual goods that are produced by their labor, taken by the capitalist and sold in the market. The workers cannot choose or keep the objects they produce, and so they do not reflect their vision.

Just think of George Michael—"frozen banana salesman/child." He doesn't keep the bananas. He dips them, freezes them, and sells them. Second, the workers are alienated from control of their own labor altogether, as the capitalist determines what is to be produced, how and why it is produced, and so on. Thus taking away the workers' ability to have free and conscious activity.

You don't imagine the working conditions in the Cornballer factory are pleasant, do you?

Third, since capitalism alienates the workers from control over their activity, and free and conscious control over that activity is the human essence, capitalism alienates the workers from their essence. Lupe probably wouldn't choose to clean Lucille Bluth's home if she didn't have to. Finally, the workers are alienated from others, and from community.

Because a worker is alienated from who he really is, his true essence, he is incapable of seeing the true essence of any other person. Just think of the office and family politics at the Bluth Company. All individuals have a creative potential, a vision, a capability of changing the world to meet this vision and the needs of others (even Lindsay). But if someone cannot see that in himself, he cannot see it as a universal property in other people.

The Bluths are a classy bunch, but instead of being "classy" in the way that means "having good taste." They're "classy" in that they're "of a class"—they're capitalists. Briefly, a class is a group of people sharing a particular relationship to the "means of production" (meaning tools and raw materials, i.e., the stuff we use when we make more stuff) in society. The two main classes in capitalism are the capitalists (also called the bourgeoise, who own the means of production and control labor) and the workers (also called the proletariat, who don't own the means of production, and are controlled as labor). Classes cause individuals of one class to see those of the other class as either resources to be used and controlled or oppressors to be feared, revered, or hated. Thus, class-based societies divide people from each other and further alienate them from community.

Perhaps surprisingly, the system of capitalism doesn't just alienate workers; it alienates capitalists, too. Marx notes that "the propertied class and the class of the proletariat represent the same human self-alienation," the difference being that "the former feels comfortable and confirmed in this self-alienation, knowing that this alienation is *its own power* and possessing it in the *semblance* of a human existence."[2] Capitalists must follow profits, rather than follow whatever goals, dreams, or passions they might otherwise have, or else other profit-motivated capitalists (like Sitwell) would quickly surpass them, and they would cease to remain capitalists.

Although capitalists do have control over the products and processes of labor, if they want to remain capitalists and not be surpassed by their competitors, then they must use their control over products to distribute goods only where profits can be made, and try to minimize labor costs while maximizing the goods laborers produce—which sounds exactly like the Bluths. The capitalist system forces capitalists to control laborers as resources and aim their own activities towards those that ultimately (even if indirectly) increase profitability.

A Case of "Light Treason": A Man Who Would Do Anything to Make a Buck

The Bluths have so many flaws it would take a TV series, a movie, and an entire book (much like the one you're holding now—thanks, by the way) to show them all. So I'll be selective (those capitalist editors are only giving me so many pages, after all). If I don't mention your favorite Bluth family secret, blame capitalism.

George Sr. has two roles within the show. First, he is a capitalist, CEO of a publicly traded company he founded (before his arrest, that is), and second, he is a father. Since opening his frozen banana stand in the 1960s, George has been used to having control in all facets of his life. And his position in capitalism, having control over the labor of others, has accustomed him to having power. It's not surprising, then, that after legally losing control, George still attempts to run the family and the company from wherever he is, be it jail or the attic of the model home. After his time as CEO (which had either created his control tendencies or amplified them), he is habitually unable to release this control, a trait that causes a lot of tension between himself and his family, most notably Michael.

As a capitalist, George Sr. sees things in terms of success (measured by profitability) and failure. George Sr.'s highly competitive and hard-to-please nature shows itself in how little approval he gives his family, especially his sons Gob, Michael, and Buster. Just think of how he manipulated his children to fight each other and then sold it as the video series *Boyfights* along with "Baby Buster" clips. A typical capitalist, George Sr. defended *Boyfights* by saying he thought it would foster a competitive spirit in his sons. George's capitalist habit of seeing things in terms of their profitability even results in commodifying himself—that is, he makes himself into an object to be sold in the capitalist marketplace. We see this in his incarceration and first religious conversion, sold as the video series *Caged Wisdom*. George Sr.'s obsession with profitability also leads him to create things simply to be sold, despite the fact that these things are basically worthless, such as his fall-apart mini-mansions and the Cornballer. Lastly, consider that George Sr. cheats on his wife, and for the sex alone (as the incarcerated George Sr. says to his son, "Daddy horny, Michael"). This attitude, too, can be seen as a result of class society. George Sr. sees women as potential objects, things-to-be-had, and he lives to consume them.

George's socioeconomic role as a capitalist manifests itself in (1) his pathological inability to give up control (even when it strains his relationship with his children, such as his manipulation of his sons to fight each other for *Boyfights*), (2) his highly competitive nature (which also damages their relationships, again revealed by the *Boyfights* fiasco), (3) his commodification of all aspects of himself and his family (showing that he views himself as only a tool for his own profit making and not as an objectively valuable person), (4) his creating things to be profitable rather than to have pride in creating things well, and

(5) his persistent womanizing, revealed by his sleeping with Kitty *despite* thinking of her as crazy. In fact, even George Sr.'s troubles with the law (and not just in Judge Reinhold's courtroom) stem from his violation of other capitalist's privileges. The Bluth Company is publicly traded, and thus when he uses company money as personal money, he is stealing the money of the other owners, other capitalists. Additionally, he gets in trouble with the U.S. government for selling mini-mansions to Saddam Hussein, violating the international-relations policies of his country (where his country's duty is to secure the privileges of its domestic capitalists). As Marx would predict, George Sr. does not actively experience his alienation from his family or himself because such separation brings him power and money. Nonetheless, he manifests alienation from both his true self (which could act in a way not dictated by profitability and competition) and in his interpersonal relationships.

Lucille and Gob

Lucille Bluth is George Sr.'s wife and co-chair of the Bluth Company, always holding at least as much power in the family and company as George Sr. Like George Sr., Lucille's relationships are defined in terms of power and control. She manipulates her children, plays them against each other, and gets pleasure from withholding love and benefits from them. Her need to dominate also causes her to compete with and hate perhaps her only possible friend, Lucille 2.

Lucille is more concerned with her appearance to others than her actual character and personal development. Her superficial materialism manifests itself in lavish spending and an extravagant lifestyle. *Conspicuous consumption* (a term from the American non-Marxist economist Veblen, not Marx) as a sign of luxury is a sign in any class-based society of being among the ruling class, those who are not only wealthy but who can afford to live impractically. Lucille's negative traits, resulting from or supported by capitalism and her class position, alienate her from her relationships with family and potential friends. In short, Lucille's negative traits reveal alienation from an independent and free, conscious self, caused or supported by the capitalist system. It's no wonder she drinks.

George Oscar Bluth (Gob, for short) is a Segway-riding former professional magician, co-founder of the Magician's Alliance, a group blackballing any magicians who reveal the secrets of tricks (although Gob would correct me for saying "tricks" rather than "illusions," because, to him, "a trick is something a whore does for money"). Of course, he was black-balled himself after a news reporter revealed how a trick of his was performed. Since then, Gob has tried to get back into the Magicians' Alliance while sometimes finding other work. Though his occupation as an entertainer would make him, in essence, a human commodity, Gob has benefited from the wealth of his family. Having an entertainment job that requires no expertise in *anything* practical (and the same can be said for his other early job, a stripper with Hot Cops), Gob is good at nothing at all. He messes things up so frequently that his tagline has become, "I've made a huge mistake." Gob is absolutely impotent in practical affairs, a direct result of the division of labor in the capitalist system, keeping individuals like Gob to one fine-tuned and specific job rather than letting them gain experience in all walks of life.

Throughout Season 2, Gob is given name-only presidency of the company from his brother Michael (who has no problem with that) while Michael is being investigated for connections to the company's illegal activities. While Gob's power is in name only, he becomes immediately power hungry and demeaning to his employees. As president, Gob wears his father's suits and does whatever he wants, at anyone's expense. Gob instantly sees employees as resources rather than people when he wears the president's suit and finds himself in the shoes of the ruling class. When asked if he wants help taking alcohol to an office party, Gob responds "No, Al, I want to spill booze all over my f**king

$6,300 suit. C'mon!!" The division of labor alienates Gob from his potential and from other people.

Meet the Fünkes

Lindsay Fünke, daughter of George Sr. and Lucille, wife of Tobias Fünke, and mother of Maeby Fünke, has benefited from her parents' wealth, too. She has lived luxuriously off the family money without ever having a steady job. In the course of the show, she has tried her hand at being an actress, an administrative assistant, a maid, a musician, and a saleswoman at a clothing store, among other things, and all without success. She even dropped out of college because she "had a job, what was the point?" This "job," of course, amounted to being paid by the Bluth Company for doing nothing. Her marriage with Tobias is beset by problems, as Tobias is a failed "analrapist" (analyst and therapist), a successful never-nude (he is psychologically incapable of being naked), and, quite possibly, a closeted homosexual—problems she tries to solve with an unsuccessful open marriage.

Lindsay shares many traits with her family members. Like her mother, she is more concerned with her public appearance than her character. (For example, she throws charity galas for social causes that she doesn't care about in order to raise her social standing.) She is a neglectful mother, sometimes forgetting her daughter entirely. Like Gob, she has tried much, and been good at almost nothing, but whereas in Gob's case it is likely from a strong division of labor combined with low natural capacity and no support, for Lindsay it is predominantly from a combination of no natural capacity, support, or attempt to be excellent to begin with. Lindsay has bought into the ideology of capitalism so thoroughly that she has no *real* passions or causes—she raises her status and consumes lavishly to make up for her marital unhappiness and meaningless existence. In short, Lindsay is entirely focused on *having* and not focused on *being* at all—the most alienated of existences.

When we first meet Tobias Fünke, he is a recently unemployed "analrapist" who lost his medical license for administering CPR to someone who didn't need it. Tobias decided to try his hand at acting, then later as an understudy for the Blue Man Group (although he originally joined because he thought they were a group of sad men). He also has stints as a security guard, owner of The Queen Mary, co-founder of Gobias Industries (with Gob), and other minor jobs. Tobias's main difficulties stem from his phobia of being naked (ruining his relationship with his wife), his repressed homosexuality (which is not explicitly confirmed but likely *also* is ruining his relationship with his wife), and his lack of skill in his newfound career of acting.

In *The Origin of the Family, Private Property, and the State*, Friedrich Engels (1820–1895), Marx's friend and collaborator, argues that the monogamous nuclear family developed to give a smooth line of inheritance for private property. Engels describes this process as resulting in the oppression of women as a sex. If this theory of the origin of the heterosexual nuclear family is true, then a Marxist *should* conclude something along the lines that homophobia is a reaction to a relationship (man to man or woman to woman) that makes patriarchal relationships and inheritance norms problematic. This would codify itself in a social aversion to homosexuality (which is actually a natural phenomenon) and imbed itself deeply in social thought, especially religion. In short, Tobias's repressed sexuality (and perhaps his phobia of being naked, stemming from subconscious discomfort with himself) can be seen as the result of private property–based economic systems (in this case, capitalism). His alienation from his true sexual identity can thus be attributed to capitalism.

Michael

Michael is the most rational and self-sacrificing character in the show, and takes over the presidency from his father (except in Season 2, where he is vice president . . . but let's be honest—he's *still* president, Gob's just sitting in his chair). Despite all this, Michael still exhibits a desire for too much control in situations and in his relationships.

Thanks to his personal moral code, Michael is far more functional and successful than any of the other Bluths. He tries to be a good father to George Michael, a good son to his parents, a good brother to his siblings, a good manager to his employees. In fact, he spends the whole show trying to save his family and their business—except, of course, for the few times he tries to leave his crazy family entirely (but who can blame him?). He is not an alcoholic or a womanizer, and he does not let his desire for too much control (which may or may not be necessary with a family so crazy) become pathological (like his father) or passive-aggressive (like his mother).

At the same time, Michael, good as he is personally, is forced in his attempts to save the family business to view the world in terms of profitability, success, and failure. This is a view that has been pushed on him by his disapproving father, himself judging the world and his sons by that standard. As a result, Michael is too self-conscious and too self-critical and has difficulties finding a relationship after the death of his wife (it's always "too soon" or "bad for George Michael"). And despite the fact that he sees his father for what he is, Michael still seeks his approval.

In short, Michael's worldview (which he struggles against) is the product of alienation produced by the capitalist system. He adopts a set of priorities that don't suit him personally. Indeed, he doesn't seem to have the choice to see the world in any other terms if he wants to save his family.

Don't Buy This Book! Down with Capitalism!

But what can the Bluths, or anyone for that matter, do to break the cycle? First, the Bluths (and anyone living under capitalism) need to look closely at the traits and values they have, social relationships they are in, and how they behave in different social roles. They need to examine these in terms of authenticity, and whether they are ultimately more helpful to themselves *and* others, or not. Second, the Bluths need to reflect on how the harmful traits, values, relationships, and so on embed themselves in their actions and choices—they need to see the web of effects. Third, they need to be committed to overcoming these harmful traits on a personal level while also looking for the ways in which society promotes these traits. The Bluths might then become committed to fighting for a socioeconomic system that struggles against these traits rather than one that is built on them.

Let's be blunt: the Bluths need to be committed to overcoming capitalism in favor of a democratic socialism, in which all people have control over their lives and share equal control over their society.

Toward the end of the series, the dysfunctional Bluths become increasingly caricatures of themselves: The more they try to fix their alienation within the system, the more disfigured and alienated they become. Such is the fate of *any* attempt at change that stops short of the heart of the matter. The volume of their absurdity, the very reason why *Arrested Development* is funny, grows in a manner that shows us one thing: alienation can only be solved by a radical departure from the way things have been done, and any attempt to solve our social problems within the system can end up only one way: hopelessly absurd. In the lives of the Bluths, this is hilarious. In our own lives, however, it all too common—and all too tragic.

NOTES

1. Karl Marx, "Economic and Philosophical Manuscripts." *Early Writings*, trans. Benton, Gregor and Rodney Livingstone. (New York: Penguin Putnam Inc., 1992), p. 328.

2. Karl Marx, "The Holy Family," *Writings of the Young Marx on Philosophy and Society.* ed. Loyd D. Easton and Kurt H. Guddat (Garden City, NY: Anchor Books, 1967), p. 367.

FAMILY FIRST

How *Not* to Run a Business

Brett Gaul

"What comes before anything? What have we always said is the most important thing?" Michael asks George Michael in the pilot of *Arrested Development*. "Breakfast," replies George Michael. "Family," says Michael. If the Bluth Company has a mission statement, it has to be "Family First." Of course, the motto is also used to justify everything from George Sr.'s having sex with Lucille in a conjugal trailer before he visits Kitty in a different conjugal trailer ("Visiting Ours") to George Michael's scoring some weed for Buster ("Pier Pressure"). But let's narrow our focus to how the motto shapes the Bluth Company's business decisions.

According to the Bluth Company's "Family First" model, a company should always do whatever is in the best interest of the family who owns the largest share of the business, regardless of whether it's legal or moral. This comes close to the classical theory of corporate social responsibility, according to which, the purpose of the corporation is to legally maximize profits for stockholders. On this account, if something's not illegal, it's permissible.[1] Rightly or wrongly, Wal-Mart has been perceived as epitomizing this model of corporate responsibility. And because some have thought that the classical theory of corporate responsibility is too narrow, a much broader alternative has been developed—the stakeholder theory. The stakeholder model—an updated corporate social responsibility with an emphasis on the *social* aspect—doesn't deny that corporations have a responsibility to look out for stockholders' interests, but it adds that corporations also have responsibilities to those with a stake in their business decisions, such as employees, customers, suppliers, and communities.[2] Johnson & Johnson's mission statement is an excellent example of the stakeholder model.[3] What Johnson & Johnson calls "Our Credo" starts by saying that the company's first responsibility is to the people who use its products. Its second responsibility is to employees, and its third responsibility is to the communities in which they work and live. Johnson & Johnson asserts that its final responsibility is to its stockholders. Clearly, the Bluth Company's "Family First" motto is much more like Wal-Mart's theory of corporate social responsibility than Johnson & Johnson's.

Product Safety: The Cornballer

Corporations have an obligation to design and sell safe products. Because the Bluth Company puts "Family First," however, the company doesn't care whether the products it sells are safe. The only concern is whether a product will make the family money. If it'll make a buck, the Bluth Company will sell it. Consider the Cornballer, a Bluth Company device that deep-fat fries cornballs. There's a problem with the product design; it gets very hot and can cause severe burns. The Cornballer is first mentioned in "Bringing Up Buster," where we see a 1970s infomercial clip in which George Sr. attacks Richard Simmons after Simmons splashes hot oil on George Sr. while removing a cornball. Later in the series Michael and Tobias also get burned by the Cornballer. Because the Cornballer is unsafe, it is illegal to sell. Upon seeing the Cornballer, Gob remarks, "I thought these were only legal in Mexico." At which point the narrator reveals that the Cornballer is actually not legal anywhere, but that George Sr. nevertheless markets the product successfully in Mexico.

In "The One Where They Build a House," George Sr. evades U.S. law enforcement by fleeing to Mexico. Mexican police mistake George Sr. for his twin brother Oscar—who is wanted in Mexico on marijuana charges—and arrest him. The police officers recognize George Sr. as the man from the Cornballer infomercial that airs in Mexico in Spanish (dubbed so that George's angry outburst is changed to "I'm crazy for these cornballs!," further illustrating the Bluth commitment to deceiving the consumer—Family First!). Each of the police officers has a large scar on his arm from being burned by the Cornballer. George Sr. avoids retribution by bribing them to say that he's dead. Two episodes later in "Good Grief!" a political cartoon titled "Frito Bandito" in a Mexican newspaper depicts George Sr. sitting on a deep-fat fry utensil being lowered into a Cornballer by a hand that has "MEXICO" written on the thumb. Apparently Mexicans weren't too impressed with the Bluth Company's Cornballer. In "Righteous Brothers," the Cornballer maims again. This time Oscar's fingerprints are burned off when he grabs the device with both hands. Having no fingerprints then makes it difficult for Oscar to prove to U.S. law enforcement that they've got the wrong man in custody after he's mistaken for George Sr.

Marketing Ethics: The Model Home

"Family First" also impacts the Bluth Company's marketing ethics. The issue here is the use of deceptive advertising tactics in the marketing of homes designed and built by the Bluth Company. Deceptive advertising is wrong because it is disrespectful and unfair to consumers. To market its homes, the company builds model homes. Potential homebuyers tour model homes, and, if they like a particular model enough, they enter into an agreement with the homebuilder to build that style of house. New homeowners don't get the house they tour, but instead get a new home of the same model. Given this, homebuilders may not want to give a model home the same level of care and attention they would give an actual home. After all, the new homeowners will be living in a new home, not the model home. However, in a subdivision like the Sudden Valley development depicted in *Arrested Development*, even the model home will eventually be sold. So the Bluths shouldn't cut too many corners in building a model home. Moreover, if the quality of a homebuilder's model homes are poor, one wonders how that builder will sell any homes at all. If the builder can't even build a decent model home, why should a potential buyer be confident that the builder can build a decent actual home? Consequently, there are very good reasons to build model homes with the same level of care and attention that would be given to actual homes. Unfortunately, these reasons are lost on the Bluth Company.

Bluth homes are first criticized in "Key Decisions" when environmental activist Johnny Bark camps out in a tree on land owned by the Bluth Company to protest the company's decision to rip out some trees to make room for more homes. Michael hears about the protestor from the local Fox affiliate. As he's watching television in the model home, a reporter states that Bark is protesting "the expansion of high-cost, low-quality mini-mansions, like this one here." The reporter then taps on the living room window of the house Michael is in and breaks the window. As the series progresses, the Bluths learn that the model home in which Michael, George Michael, Tobias, Lindsay, and Maeby live is poorly built. In "Let 'Em Eat Cake"

George Michael accidentally knocks off a piece of the balcony railing. "Buddy, you got to take it easy, okay?" says Michael, "I'm showing this as the model again. I don't want people to think we have shoddy workmanship." As soon as Michael says this, a piece of wood falls off the television cabinet and bumps a speaker, knocking it off the wall. "That might not have been your fault," he says to George Michael. Later in the same episode a knob falls off a kitchen cabinet and Tobias breaks the handle on the oven door. "That doesn't inspire confidence," says Lindsay.

In "Switch Hitter," more things go wrong with the house. The same piece of wood falls off the television cabinet again, and Tobias leans on the refrigerator and moves it backward a few feet. "Don't worry," he says, "it has not fallen into the garage. Knock on wood." Tobias then proceeds to knock on the wall, at which point the refrigerator does fall into the garage. Later George Sr. thumps the attic wall with his fist, causing the oven's overhead vent to fall on Lindsay's foot. Fortunately, Lindsay is so loaded up on Teamocil that she doesn't even notice that her foot is bleeding. In "Righteous Brothers" Michael discovers that the model home is sinking because the drain pipes aren't hooked up. They just empty under the house. All that's down there, a housing inspector tells Michael, is a lot of blue paint and some denim—remnants of Tobias's Blue Man Group dreams and his never-nude ways.

While the original model home might deceive potential homebuyers into thinking that the Bluth Company builds quality homes, the Bluths engage in a similar form of deception in "The One Where They Build a House," the episode in which they build a second model home to make it look like the company is doing well. Michael thinks they can build the home within two months, but Gob, who at the time is serving as the president of the company, demands that they do it in just two weeks. Given their severe time constraints, Michael tells his crew of George Michael, Buster, Oscar, and actor Tom Jane from the movies *Homeless Dad* and *Junk* ("They Shoot Heroin, Don't They?"), that the house "doesn't have to be good, it just has to look good." All that this inexperienced crew manages to build in two weeks is the outside of the house, which falls down at the ribbon cutting ceremony, revealing that neither the house nor the Bluth Company is "Solid as a Rock" despite what Starla, Gob's "business model," suggests.

In "Mr. F," Gob attempts to fool Japanese investors—who may have heard that the development site has a mole problem—by building a miniature city outside a window of the original model home and telling them that it's far away. "It'll look real if you squint," promises Gob. "God knows they're squinters." The Bluths are worried that these badly needed investors will back out once they realize that the company hasn't built anything. Just as Gob is showing the financiers the fake housing development, Tobias, wearing a mole costume (because he thinks he's auditioning for a role as a mole) starts rampaging the tiny town in front of the horrified investors. At this point a jetpack-wearing George Michael enters the picture and knocks down the giant mole a few times. "I ache with embarrassment," says one of the Japanese investors, who were never heard from again.

Treatment of Employees: The Banana Stand and Child Labor

"Family First" is sadly reflected in the company's treatment of employees. Time and time again we see the Bluth Company treating employees poorly so that the company can make a buck, beginning with Bluth's Original Frozen Banana Stand. Contrary to the name, the idea for such a stand was not "original" with the Bluths. Although George Sr. started the banana stand in 1953, the series finale reveals that he and Lucille stole the idea from a Korean businessman and had him deported. Annyong, that Korean businessman's grandson, would later come to live with Lucille, who adopts Annyong because she thinks the company could use some good publicity—and to teach Buster a lesson, because he won't finish his cottage cheese.

As we know, the banana stand often employs Bluth children. George Michael spends a lot of time there, sometimes with help from his cousin Maeby—who is also later employed as a film executive for Tantamount Studios. In fact, in the pilot George Michael is introduced as "Frozen banana salesman/child." And Michael often worked at the banana stand as a kid, too. In "Top Banana" we see a clip of hot, overwhelmed, and young Michael apparently working the stand by himself. He has chocolate on his forehead and cheek and sweat pouring down his face; the line of customers is long; and he looks like he desperately needs a break and some help. In that same episode, George Michael tells Michael that he'd like to work more hours at the banana stand. George Michael wants to work more because his attraction to Maeby is dominating his thoughts, and he thinks some time away from her will quell his incestuous desires. Unfortunately for George Michael, his father makes Maeby join him in the banana stand so that she can learn the value of work—something she can't learn from her unemployed parents. Michael makes George Michael the manager (Mr. Manager, but we just say, "manager" . . .) of the banana stand and offers his son the following advice for managing his new employee: "You stay on top of her, buddy. Do not be afraid to ride her. Hard."

Besides the fact that working in the banana stand with Maeby makes George Michael uncomfortable, there's a problem with having children work there at all. Both Michael and Maeby are under sixteen years old, and U.S. child labor laws place significant restrictions on the number of hours they can work.[4] The Bluth Company probably violates child labor laws again in "Staff Infection" when Lucille says Annyong—whose "work ethic is unbelievable"—is heading off to work a ten-hour shift at the banana stand. I say "probably" here because no one really knows how old Annyong is. Lucille does call him a "young boy," however. Perhaps using so much child labor is the reason why at the end of "Top Banana" Michael realizes that the banana stand is the only profitable part of the Bluth Company. And if you're going to break the law so that the family can make some money, why not put family—especially young family—to work first?

The banana stand isn't the only money-making venture in which the Bluth Company exploits children, though. In "Making a Stand" we learn that George Sr. provoked his sons to fight one another and then taped these fights—which were popular in Latin America—and sold copies under the name *Boyfights*. The *Boyfights* series included the titles "Boyfights: A Day in the Life of American Boys," with bonus footage of Baby Buster in "I Don't Want to Go to Bed"; "Boyfights 2: Boys Will Be Boys," with bonus footage of Baby Buster in "Too Old to Breastfeed"; "A Boyfights Cookout," featuring "Run for Your Life!" with bonus footage of Baby Buster in "A Fifth Grader Wets His Bed"; and "Backseat Boyfights: The Trip to Uncle Jack's 70th," with bonus footage of Crybaby Buster in "I Don't Want to Be on This Tape!"

Treatment of Employees: The Office and the Construction Site

The Bluth Company's poor treatment of employees using the "Family First" motto isn't limited to the banana stand—it permeates every aspect of the company, including the office and the construction site. In the realm of the office, consider Gob at the company Christmas party in "Afternoon Delight," in which he alienates employees by constantly referring to his expensive suit, which, he tells different people at various points in the episode, is valued at $3,000, $4,000, $5,000, $6,300, and finally $3,600 (for the pants alone). Then, at the Christmas party, Gob fires all of the employees for laughing when Tom—whom George Sr. had once fired at a previous Christmas party for joking that the company's numbers haven't been adding up because "George has been into the kitty" (an obvious reference to George's Sr. affair with his secretary Kitty)—toasts Gob by reluctantly saying that "Gob seems like he'd be a really smart boss" and that "he's a great magician." As some consolation, the next day Michael throws another Christmas party for the employees at the banana stand to assure them that they have not really been fired.

The Bluth Company motto of "Family First" is also illustrated in "Staff Infection" when Michael wants construction site workers to work without pay. The company is behind on payroll and won't have any money to pay its employees until the zoning committee gives its approval to the Bluth Company's plans for a new subdivision. It's a Saturday, and Michael advises the foreman to "keep [his] head down, power through, you know, and sacrifice." Because the Bluth Company puts "Family First," Michael has no qualms about making employees sacrifice on a sunny weekend for the sake of the family.

International Business: "Light" Treason

The Bluth Company's "Family First" motto gets them into trouble with the CIA—well, at least the CIA East—when George Sr. makes a deal to build homes in Iraq. Because U.S. corporations have been prohibited from doing business with Iraq since the early 1990s, George Sr. says that he may be guilty of some "light" treason. In "Exit Strategy" we learn that, unbeknownst to the CIA East, the CIA West—which shares the other side of a cubicle with the CIA East—had helped set up a deal in which the Bluth Company built homes in Iraq for Saddam Hussein. The CIA West arranged this so that they could wire the homes with listening devices in the hopes of learning if and where Saddam had weapons of mass destruction. The Bluths, CIA East agent Richard Shaw says, are "unintentional operations victims." "We feel terrible," he later adds, "because this is really our mistake."

Of course, the Bluth-built Iraqi homes have some of the same problems as the shoddily built U.S. model home. In "Let 'Em Eat Cake" a television reporter in Iraq reports from one of Saddam's mini-palaces; the palace looks just like the "Seawind unit" the Bluths live in and even has some of the same furnishings. As the reporter is explaining that U.S. troops are living in some of these houses, a soldier knocks off the same part of the balcony railing that George Michael did in the U.S. model home earlier in the episode. The reporter notes that the home has sustained a lot of damage, but that most of it is due to "shoddy workmanship."

Moral Development Arrested

By putting themselves before the people who use their products, their employees, and their community, the Bluth Company often makes unethical decisions at the expense of others. Typically, their immoral behavior results in only a short-term benefit, which is soon wiped out by the long-term consequences created by the same behavior. Although it turns out that George Sr. is not guilty of treason—light or otherwise—the company has other problems concerning shady bookkeeping and defrauding investors. While George Sr. is innocent of wrongdoing in building homes in Iraq, he appears guilty of various SEC violations. Seeing the authorities coming to get him, George Sr. calls the office and tells them to "empty the account" and start shredding documents. He later tells Michael that the SEC has been after him for years. From watching the pilot alone we can see why someone might have tipped off the SEC about the Bluth Company—most of the Bluth family uses the company's bank account as their own.

In the series finale "Development Arrested," we learn that even though George Sr. is not innocent, the embezzlement and pension robbing charges against him, like the treason charges, have been dropped. Just when it appears that the Bluth Company's unethical ways are going to go unpunished, the SEC swoops in again. This time the charges are against Lucille, who was named CEO of the Bluth Company in the pilot. While George Sr. has been in prison, Annyong has been amassing evidence of Lucille's wrongdoing in an attempt to bring down the Bluth family and exact revenge for his deported grandfather.

Throughout the series, Michael knows that the family's business philosophy is seriously flawed, but he never follows through with his repeated threats to leave the family and the company because he desperately seeks his father's approval. In "S.O.B.s" the family throws a Save Our Bluths legal defense fundraiser. During a speech at the event Michael admits that "maybe the Bluths aren't worth saving" and that they're "very self-centered." "Anyway," he concludes, "here's my advice to you. Go ahead and take yourself a goody bag and get out of here while you still can." If Michael really wanted to run an ethical business—as he professes a number of times that he does—he should've heeded his own advice or modified the family motto. Following the Bluth Company's "Family First" credo only results in having one's moral development arrested. In short, what we learn from the Bluth Company is how *not* to run a business.

NOTES

1. For a defense of the classical model of social responsibility, see Milton Friedman's "The Social Responsibility of Business Is to Increase Its Profits," in *The New York Times Magazine* (September 13, 1970). Milton's article is also reprinted in *Contemporary Issues in Business Ethics.* 4th ed. Edited by Joseph R. DesJardins and John McCall (Belmont, CA: Wadsworth Publishing, 2000), p. 9.

2. Further explanation of the stakeholder model is provided by R. Edward Freeman's *Strategic Management: A Stakeholder Approach* (Marshfield, MA: Pitman, 1984).

3. Johnson & Johnson's credo can be viewed online at http://www.jnj.com/wps/wcm/connect/30e290804ae70eb4bc4afc0f0a50cff8/our-credo.pdf?MOD=AJPERES (accessed June 30, 2009).

4. According to U.S. child labor laws, fourteen- and fifteen-year-olds can only work outside of school hours from 7:00 A.M. to 7:00 P.M. From June 1 through Labor Day, though, they can work until 9:00 P.M. Fourteen- and fifteen-year-old workers can also work no more than three hours on a school day, eighteen hours in a school week, eight hours on a non-school day, and forty hours in a non-school week. There are no restrictions on the work hours of those sixteen years old and older, however. They can work any day, any time of day, and for any number of hours. For more information about U.S. child labor laws, see the Department of Labor's website, especially the page found at http://www.youthrules.dol.gov/hours.htm.

BOURGEOIS BLUTHS

Arrested Development
and Class Status

Rachel McKinney

From yachts to designer clothes, from private schools to lavishly catered parties, the Bluths lead privileged lives. Indeed, the excesses of American capitalism are one of the main targets of *Arrested Development's* satire. But how exactly does the show represent socioeconomic class as a social category? What can we learn about class status, anxiety, consumption, labor, and the family by inquiring into the politics of our favorite dysfunctional clan? What does it mean to be bourgeois and a Bluth?

Your Uncle Doesn't Not Work Here
Anymore: Marx, Labor, and Capital

To begin, a crash course in terminology might be helpful. For Karl Marx (1818–1883), under conditions of capitalism, society is divided into two main social groups: those who own and control the means of production (the bourgeoisie) and those whose labor fuels this production (the proletariat). Under capitalism, labor becomes a commodity to be bought and sold in the marketplace. Because the only thing available to members of the proletariat is their own labor, the only option available for subsistence for the working class is the sale of this labor for wages. This labor is then converted into more capital as the worker produces goods and services. The bourgeoisie then sells the products of this labor in the marketplace, making a substantial profit. By keeping wages low, the owners of the means of production can pay workers just enough for basic necessities—in the traditional formulation, enough for the head of household to sustain his home life and provide for the next generation of workers, his children. The bourgeoisie take surplus value from sales of the goods and services and either reinvests the profits or uses them for their own purposes.

Marx's two-category taxonomy doesn't easily map on to our contemporary American English use of terms categorizing social class. In casual conversation, the terms *bourgeois*, *poor*, and *middle-class* pick out lots of different things. In addition to a person's relationship to the means of production (what Marx was primarily interested in), we track social practices, social position, wealth, education, access to resources, and even geographical location. While it's true that the Bluths do own the means of production—the process of producing McMansions for wealthy southern Californian suburbanites— they are situated as "bourgeois" beyond this mere fact. Their status, wealth, and practical activities all serve to make them recognizably members of the bourgeoisie. Because of these factors, I'll be taking a wide scope when using the term *bourgeois*, discussing several factors of the Bluth's lives that situate them as members of a capital-owning elite.

It's a Gaming Ship:
Consumption and Leisure

While for Marx bourgeois identity is primarily marked by one's status as a member of a capital-owning class, within the world of the Bluths we see bourgeois identity in the practices of consumption and leisure. What the Bluths buy—expensive conditioner and diamond dust crème (Lindsay), furs and jewelry (Lucille), $5000 suits—C'mon! (George Sr. and later Gob)—as well as how they buy it (at expensive boutiques, the most exclusive hotels and restaurants)—are a means of making visible the wealth (or illusion of wealth) they have. Indeed, their consumption reveals a preoccupation with frivolity: the Bluths, in the words of Dorothy Parker (1893–1967), are only interested in taking care of the luxuries and expect the necessities to take care of themselves.

The Bluths are masters at offering reasonable-sounding justifications for their unreasonable purchases. When George Sr. buys a hot tub for the attic, both for his aches and to provide a method for cooking dinner, he can't fathom that this purchase might be a poor, short-sighted investment. Indeed, the attic didn't turn out to be the "party hang-out" that he had envisioned.

The way the Bluths spend their time also identifies their class status. While daily work clutters our lives, the Bluths' days are filled with leisure. Constant parties at Lucille's townhouse that celebrate events not worth celebrating ("You're killing me, buster"), Spring Breaking for weeks at a time (and referring to this time of year as "the holidays"), shopping sprees and fancy restaurants, all these things contribute to a life spent playing hard rather than working hard. Indeed, even the Bluths' labor practices (what they do for work) *look* like leisure practices (what the rest of us do for play). Tobias's acting career, Buster's years as a graduate student and areas of study (cartography? Native American tribal ceremonies?), and Gob's magic tricks (or rather, *illusions*) don't really provide a wage or fulfill a social need. The Bluths engage in low-stakes, low-responsibility activity subsidized by the family's considerable assets. To top it off, many times these activities are illegal (the family's shoplifting in "Not Without My Daughter"), destructive (Gob blowing up the yacht in "Missing Kitty"), and immoral (just think of all the doves, rabbits, and chickens who have sacrificed their lives for Gob's magic shows).

The Bluths' relationship to real labor is equally troubling. During the Bluth Company's crunch time on a new housing development, it comes to Michael's attention that his mother and siblings have been receiving paychecks for years without doing any work for the company. To remedy this, Michael puts Lindsay in charge of the office and Buster and Gob on the construction site. The only family member who finds that he enjoys manual labor is Buster, and even then it's because the process offers him a sense of novelty and whimsical camaraderie ("I love it here! And the *language* these guys use! *Rough.* One of these guys told me to take my head out of my *bottom* and get back to work. My *bottom*!"). Meanwhile, when Gob takes up the workers' plight as his own and organizes a work stoppage, Lindsay retaliates by presenting Lupe's family (who thought they were being taken on a vacation trip to Catalina) as scabs. Seeing the Bluths forced to work for the first time in their lives quickly turns into watching them do everything they can to avoid *actually* working. These shenanigans are the privilege of privilege: if the Bluths were working class—or even middle class—they wouldn't have the choice of "opting out" of labor practices in the ways that they do. Indeed, if we think about who in the show actually does work, we find that the answer is: children (George Michael at the banana stand, Maeby at the movie studio), women of color (Lupe and her family), machines (the Roomba that replaces Lupe), and sometimes—*sometimes*—Michael.

There's Always Money in the Banana Stand: Class Status and Performance

The characters of *Arrested Development* are never quite sure where they stand. Consider Tom Jane—the famous actor that Lindsay meets while he is slumming as a homeless man to research a movie role. Tom Jane is an interesting counterpoint to the Bluths. Lindsay meets him outside of a bar, assuming him to be a casually dressed celebrity (he had the effortless, dressed down look of a movie star, anyway). Then, walking into a liquor store, the clerk tells them he doesn't allow homeless people in the store, and Lindsay is immediately repulsed. Of course, we later find out that Jane has affected the trappings of homelessness in order to further his goals (in this case, to study for an acting role). This incident shows that one of the ways in which social class becomes recognizable in *Arrested Development* is through performance. How one dresses and carries one's self, how one grooms, and the places one frequents are all ways of performing what one *wants* to be. Whereas for Lindsay and the rest of the Bluths, this performance is upward-directed, for Tom Jane's research interests it is downward-driving. While being a member of a socioeconomic class isn't just how one appears to others (after all, Jane still *is* a movie star), markers such as clothing, speech, and performance are important social signals for how other people will perceive you.

Class is also about *place*. A recurring theme of *Arrested Development* is the places that the characters do and do not occupy among Southern California's rich, powerful, and elite. The Bluths are sustained by constant attention to, and preoccupation with, their ability to gain access into the most prestigious schools (the Milford Academy and Openings), exclusive restaurants (Rudd), and other cultural institutions (the Living Classics pageant). And when it comes to public institutions such as the legal system, the Bluths expect (and indeed receive) special treatment and privilege within those institutions—George

Sr. paying off the Mexican authorities, a series of expensive (if often incompetent) private attorneys, and so on.

In fact, the game of keeping up the appearance of an aloof, privileged Southern California lifestyle is more important to the Bluths than actually developing the financial resources to sustain that lifestyle. *Passing* as upper class becomes a priority over actually *being* upper class. Needing to present themselves as part of the bourgeoisie becomes the point of intentional activity, and the result of this is a constant anxiety over class status, presentation, and identity. Consider Lucille's shock and horror upon learning that her country club membership had been downgraded to "poolside only." Her sense of revulsion is so complete that even her body responds violently: her stomach, after all, isn't "used to curly fries." What it is to be upper class is so intimately tied to what it is to present one's self as upper class that Lucille's very body can't handle the unexpected revelation that her persona and gradual "slide into poverty" is more visible than ever before.

I Thought You Meant of the Things You Eat: the Bluths and the Politics of the Family

By many standards the Bluths are a nontraditional family: Michael is a single parent, Lucille's husband is in jail, Lindsay and Tobias are separated and struggling, Gob unknowingly has a son out of wedlock, Lucille adopts (and subsequently neglects) a child across national and racial lines. Adultery is normalized and expected. Alcoholism is tolerated and encouraged (I mean, we don't want the vodka to go bad, do we?). The Bluth men fight over women (Marta, Lucille Ostero) just as they fight over toys in the *Boyfights* VHS movies (which, incidentally, were a huge hit in Mexico). They are, in many ways, the opposite of the perfect nuclear family.

And yet, these are features of family life that are a substantial part of the fabric of American reality. Single parenting like Michael's is no longer an unexpected, remarkable feature. With millions of Americans in jail, families separated by the prison system are increasingly common. Young men, like the teenaged Gob, father children without bearing the fiscal or emotional responsibilities of fatherhood. There is no question that these are problems that face, not just Americans today, but people generally. What makes these features notable is not the fact that these things are happening, but the context in which they appear. These are features of family life that we're not used to seeing portrayed on television within the upper-middle class, white So-Cal demographic, unless of course we're big fans of *The O.C.* (don't call it . . . wait, that's actually the name of the show . . .).

Michael, of course, is supposed to be the moral center of the family unit: he's the character who most explicitly takes it upon himself to keep the family together and to promote their well-being. But Michael has his own list of failings and familial betrayals. In romantic relationships, he's less than a gentleman: he steals Gob's girlfriend Marta, he culpably fails to realize Rita's mental retardation, and he seduces and lies to a (supposedly) blind woman (finally throwing a Bible at her in court in an effort to both embarrass her and get his father out of paying his debt to society). He's unable to actually listen to and communicate with his son, George Michael (and what father would give his son the name of the pop star and former lead singer of *Wham?*). Rather than supporting his son, he meddles with and dismisses George Michael's relationship with Ann ("Bland," "Egg," "Yam," "Plant"), even leaving her in a foreign country at one point.

Is Michael's devotion and commitment to family values genuine? Or, rather, are Lindsay, Gob, and Tobias's criticisms of him true: that his self-satisfaction at being the "good guy" is the driving motivation behind his actions, and that he is in fact only happy when he's needed by others? Is the Bluth family—perpetually in crisis—the only context he can thrive in?

In answering this, one point worth noticing is that much of the humor of *Arrested Development* relies on subverting our expectations of happy, functional families. Consider Dr. Fünke's 100 percent Natural Good-Time Family-Band Solution: the illusion of family togetherness, love, and stability serves as means of marketing chemical supplements with disgusting and problematic side effects ("Let's take it from 'Loose Stool'!"). The supplements—Teamocil, Euphorazine, and Xanotab—work by tranquilizing their users: they make docile bodies of volatile subjects.

For the Bluths, however, it's only with these products that the features we take to be necessary conditions of an emotionally functional family—trust, care, affection, honesty, and mutual respect—emerge. Perhaps this unrelatability, unconventionality, and unexpectedness really were factors in the show's short network television lifespan (it's not as if they didn't realize it, either!). The Bluths are not the sort of family we're *used* to seeing on TV. It's difficult to see these characters in terms of the familiar categories and roles that we've grown accustomed to seeing elsewhere in the television sitcom world. Lucille and Lindsay are not mothers in the same way as, for example, *The Simpsons'* Marge Simpson or *Family Guy's* Lois Griffin are: they don't exist as the responsible moral center, they don't offer the promise of stability and comfort, and they don't serve as mere foils to their husbands' punchlines. "If I go with you," Lindsay tells her daughter Maeby when discussing the Bluth Company's Christmas party, "it'll just make me seem like a *mother*."And while Maeby has never thought of her this way, and while this may make her—and the other Bluths—more fitting and robust comedic characters within the space of the show, it doesn't make them any more likable. The Bluths fail to be relatable *qua* (a bourgeois way of saying "as") people, but also *qua* members of a televised family unit. Whatever complications arise in real life, we expect our sitcom families to be antiseptic and emotionally nonconfrontational. This is why the Bluths both horrify and delight us.

The Important Thing Is That You Guys Don't Lose Focus on Yourselves: Narcissism as a Crisis of Bourgeois Identity

In thinking through the Bluth's social practices, anxiety about class status, and dysfunctional family ties it's worth thinking about another feature of the Bluths' psychology: namely, their relationship to themselves. They're selfish, self-centered, self-aggrandizing, and self-righteous, all without any real insight into their own inner lives or motivations. The Bluths for the most part operate without any attention to *why* they may be doing the things they do or wanting the things they want. And it isn't clear that they're interested in investigating how their behavior hooks up to the world, let alone how their actions impact those around them. A culture of narcissism permeates the Bluths's world. In addition to opting out of conventional labor and family responsibilities, they opt out of genuine human relationships whenever possible.

Consider, for example, Lindsay's self-aggrandizing political "activism" (HOOP and anti-circumcision, protesting the war in Iraq only when she finds out her hair stylist is being sent to the front, or helping Johnny Bark protect the trees near the Bluths' housing tract lot until she realizes that this entails a lack of modern plumbing). Unlike legitimate political activism that arises from homegrown struggles for equality, justice, and liberation, Lindsay's activism is born of attention seeking. When she ends up dancing in front of a crowd at a war protest (in "Whistler's Mother"), Lindsay discovers that "the activism that came out of her desire for prettier hair did in fact boost her self-esteem." Later in the series, Lindsay stops by an anti-gun protest to check out the scene, not having "picked a side" yet. Then, despite her shouts of "murderer" she is swayed by television's "Frank Wrench" and flips sides to the anti-gun-control movement. Her motivation for defending the separation of church and state, similarly, comes after she stubs her toe on a statue of the Ten Commandments at the courthouse. Lindsay is not authentically invested in the positions she defends (how can we forget this triad: "No More Meat!" "No More Fish!" and "More Meat and Fish!"?). As an outsider to these political struggles, she finds herself fulfilled by the attention she receives without actually having to hold any political, social, or ethical commitments.

Or consider the family's lack of sensitivity following Buster's seal accident. After Buster's hand gets bitten off, his mother and siblings can barely contain their disgust and resentment. They are unsympathetic to the point where even the sight of Buster—or sitting too close in the stair car—is perceived as an unreasonable burden. The Bluths lacks the simple human capacities to take the needs and desires of others—even their own kin!—into account. This narcissism—this lack of attention or care paid to others' lives and interests—functions as a *privilege*. There's something specifically bourgeois about this pathology. Because their wealth, status, and suburban location insulate them from unwanted human contact, the Bluths are afforded the luxury of spending their time worrying about themselves rather than others. The psychopathology behind Buster's panic attacks, Gob's Spring Break binges, and Tobias's time-sink acting career delusions are made possible by the Bluths's financial wherewithal. The Bluths's considerable resources enable a lifestyle of opting out of genuine human interactions. The result of this privilege—narcissism—is a siege on human communication and meaningful relationships.

What, then, can we say about the pathology structuring the Bluths' lives? How are the dsyfunctionality, narcissism, and anxiety related to their class status? This brings us back to our original discussion of the traditional definition of the *bourgeois*. Remember that Marx originally understood the term as a way of talking about that group of people who own and control the means of production. Of course, this is only part of the story. Controlling the means of production isn't all there is to being a good member of the economic elite: The good capitalist will reinvest, expand, and produce more wealth. By increasing production, reinvesting capital, keeping wages and overhead low, expanding into other markets, and further penetrating existing markets, the owners of the means of production can secure their position for years to come.

The Bluths, of course, don't do any of this. Despite Michael's best efforts, not only do they fail to grow or produce more wealth (I mean, they celebrate being *upgraded* to a "don't buy" company with a huge party!), they're constantly under threat of losing control of the company: either by being bought out by the likes of Lucille Ostero and Stan Sitwell or by being shut down by the courts. Mismanagement—financial and familial—is at the heart of the Bluths' crises. Unable to control their wealth, their anxieties, or each other, the Bluths represent a family beset by the complications and anxieties of being bourgeois.

PART THREE

SOME HUGE MISTAKES

WHAT WHITEY ISN'T READY TO HEAR

Social Identity in *Arrested Development*

J. Jeremy Wisnewski

You There, Reading This Book . . .

So you're a reader—and a fan of *Arrested Development*. A TV-watcher and a reader. I know your kind. You probably think you're some kind of intellectual, too? I mean *philosophy* . . . that's some highfalutin stuff. I'm getting a sense of what I might expect from you. You'll finish reading this sentence, you'll talk about *Arrested Development*, and you probably harbor warm feelings for Ron Howard (and who could blame you?).

I bet you've got some siblings you annoy, and who annoy you, and I bet you lost a hand to a seal a couple years ago. I also bet you've got a weird romance thing going on with your mother and that you have dabbled in cartography. You're probably even wearing cutoff jean-shorts under your pants.

Sorry. I got a little carried away there. What I'm doing is *interpreting you.* I'm taking some small fact about your actions and I'm using that small fact to figure out who you are. In this case, the only fact I've got is that you're reading these sentences—but that gives me a lot to go on. I can take that one little thing and construct a world around it—a world full of boxes to check and labels to place—a world where I know exactly what it means to be someone like you.

So, book reader, I've got you figured out. But you've got me figured out as well. I'm that snarky philosophy professor who thinks he's so cool because he likes *Arrested Development,* and who thinks he's so hip because he writes snotty little essays that directly address his readers. And right you are!

But identity isn't all fun and games. If there's anything I've learned from *Arrested Development,* it's that identities are things we can be forced into—that can blind others to who we are, or that might even blind *us* to who we are. Whether in the O.C. (don't call it that) or elsewhere, we aren't just who we want to be. We're also what others *determine* us to be. And here's the scary thing, book reader. That's how *all* identity works. We aren't simply born whole from the heads of Zeus or George Sr. We're social animals, as Aristotle (384–322 BCE) reminds us. We are the product not just of who we *think* we are, but of who, and what, *others* think we are. Identity is thus fundamentally a social enterprise. It isn't simply something one can choose. In lots of ways, our identities are things that are constantly negotiated with those around us. Because identities are negotiated—because they can be forced on us by others—they have an inherently ethical dimension.

Whatever I Do, I Won't Quote Hegel

The Canadian philosopher Charles Taylor argues that a "crucial feature of human life is its fundamentally dialogical character.

We become full human agents, capable of understanding our-selves, and hence of defining our identity, through our acquisi-tion of rich human languages of expression."[1] These "languages" aren't just the spattering of words we happen to know (if so, Annyong would be in big trouble in the Bluth household!). Taylor has in mind a much broader notion of language that captures all those things that allow us to express and define ourselves: our interests, our goals, and even our artistic and professional projects. A language, in this sense, is any systematic expression of who one is—of "where one stands." (Hell, even a commitment to the Sudden Valley Housing Development, or the Cornballer, might count.) As Taylor goes on to point out, "people do not acquire the languages needed for self-definition on their own. Rather, we are introduced to them through oth-ers who matter to us . . . the genesis of the human mind is in this sense not monological, not something each person accom-plishes on his or her own, but dialogical."[2]

Identities, then, aren't the sorts of things we can pull up by our own bootstraps, to contort an expression irresponsibly (c'mon!). To have an identity that allows a modicum of self-respect, *others* must recognize this identity as valid and fulfill-ing. This is a point the German philosopher G. W. F. Hegel (1770–1831) famously made in his *master/slave dialectic:* We can flourish as human beings only to the extent that we're recog-nized by others; such recognition is basic to human well-being. (As promised by the section title, I won't quote Hegel. His work is as difficult to read as Fünke's bestselling *The Man Inside Me,* albeit for mostly different reasons.)

The absence of recognition is the source of a lot of misery. The Bluth clan knows this all too well. Tobias, for example, wants to be recognized as a victim of a debilitating condition (never-nudity—there are literally dozens of us!). No one takes his condition seriously, however, and he's left with an identity that isn't acknowledged by the world around him. Likewise, Gob is a magician, but not one that anyone takes seriously—and not being taken seriously is a situation that is recurrent in Gob's life as much as it is in Buster's. Neither brother is regarded as *recognition-worthy* in anything they pursue. Who would call Gob a successful magician, let alone an illusionist? And let's not forget Gob's failed businesses (Bees? Beads?! We'll see who makes more honey! Bzzzz.). Who would dare to call Buster an academic with expertise in cartography ("the mapping of uncharted territories") and seventeenth-century agrarian economics ("are we at all concerned about an uprising?")? Certainly touching yourself is not a scholarly pursuit. I mean, c'mon!

But even when we're recognized by others as having an identity—as being a businessman, or an illusionist, or an academic, or an analrapist—this doesn't mean that everything's going to be hunky dory. Identity can go bad in another way: Some of the identities that we take on involve *devaluation* (It's hard to read "analrapist" in any way but a negative one, even when we change the pronunciation). In other words, being recognized as having an identity isn't enough to have a fulfilling and self-respecting existence. We've also got to be recognized as having identities that are *worth* having. And here's the big issue: *most* identities are *normative*—that is, we implicitly evaluate most of the identities that we find ourselves taking on. Lupe, Franklin, Gob, and Buster can help us see this.

It Ain't Easy Bein' White

Some of the things that make us who we are can be picked up and put down at will: You can be an *Arrested Development* fan or not; you can be an advocate of "Caged Wisdom" or you can completely ignore it. In this sense, an identity is just a way of understanding oneself. As the contemporary philosophy Georgia Warnke has claimed, identity is really a way of *interpreting* oneself.[3] As such, identities can be fun and fantastic things—they can embody our understanding of ourselves as everything from illusionists to cartographers.

But, as we've seen, identities can have a dark side, too. Identities can also "go imperial" (to borrow a turn of phrase from Warnke). Ways of being interpreted can come to dominate everything about us. *Some* ways of understanding ourselves seem to be outright forced on us. The most imperial identities—ones that force themselves on us, and are virtually impossible to escape—are race, sex, and gender.[4] No matter how hard we try, and no matter how much we want to get beyond them, race, sex, and gender are forced on us again and again, even when they don't need to be. Take the case of race. As Warnke notes, "We cannot become ex-white in the same way that we can become an ex-patriot."[5] This isn't because race is physical and nationality is not. As it turns out, race *isn't* physical (there's no way of determining race by looking at genetic make-up). Race forces itself on us because we think of it as *more essential* than nationality. So, while we accept that we can run off to live in the O.C. and become an ex-patriot of New York, we think of race as something we just can't leave behind. We *are* our race. This is the very definition of an imperial identity: no matter where we go, our race follows us.

Just to illustrate this, we might as well talk for a second about Michael Jackson. Does it matter if Michael Jackson was *really* black? Most biologists today deny that race is biologically real (there are no genetic markers for membership in a race, and there is more intraracial genetic variation than there is interracial genetic variation). This makes it seem like insisting that Michael Jackson was *really* black is just dumb, if it means anything at all. If there's no such thing as black, ole MJ couldn't *really* have been black any more than Franklin could have become "all puckered and white" (c'mon!).

And yet, we often view people as essentially being members of a particular race or ethnic group (the jury is still out on science, after all). The Bluths manage to do this more than your average family in the O.C. (I know . . . but I like calling it that). Let's think back on how the Bluths understand Mexican identity (enter eerie flashback music *or* Ron Howard narration) . . .

Despite his studies in cartography, when Buster tries to flee to Mexico, he winds up in Santa Anna, California (about six minutes inland from his house). He's totally oblivious to the fact, having no sense of what Mexico might actually be like. He crawls under a picnic table, worried about the unbearable heat of the "Mexican" sun. Buster is unaffected by reality, and entirely affected by his preconceived notions of what Mexico must be like—as well as preconceived notions about what it means to be Hispanic. He is so bound up in his preconceived notions that he doesn't even recognize Lupe as the woman who cleans his former residence! In talking to Lupe's family, Buster speaks slowly and deliberately, enunciating his sounds, and laying on the fake Mexican accent. "I'm one of you now, si?" ("Amigos"). The next day, on the way to work with his newfound family, Buster remarks, "This is great. We're like slave buddies."

Apparently, Buster thinks that being Mexican is like being a slave. But he's not entirely to blame. He grew up believing that Rosa, the old Bluth housekeeper, lived in the kitchen. When Lupe eventually leaves the Bluth's employ for having had sex with Buster, she is replaced with a robot—and no one much notices—Buster even has sex with *it* too (what do you expect, at that point he's half-machine!).

Lindsay isn't any better, and she might even be worse. She's got the hots for Ice, the African-American bounty hunter and caterer (how's that for playing with stereotypes?), but this doesn't really prove anything. Sexual attraction and racism aren't mutually exclusive. Still, we'd be better off focusing on how Lindsay treats others generally, and since we've been talking about Mexican identity, we'd do well to remember some things about sister Bluth. I know a busload of Mexicans just trying to have a reunion who would say Lindsay's got the wrong idea about what it means to be Mexican. It *doesn't* mean that one's a day laborer willing to scab on a construction site! And let's not forget that Lindsay more or less kidnaps

Lupe when she wants the model home cleaned ("Immaculate Election").

Lucille is the worst of the group in this, as in other matters. She searches Lupe's purse before Lupe can leave the house, asking, "Is this your onion?" Lucille also finds a ball of foil, and suspiciously questions Lupe as to its contents. When Lupe responds, "Nothing, it's a ball of foil for my son," Lucille allows her to go on her way. When Lucille goes to the Daytime Desi awards, she continuously asks the Hispanic guests/actors to get her a drink. Apparently, Lucille believes that Hispanics are naturally part of the service industry—that to be Hispanic is just to be someone who waits on whitey. She even says as much: "A room full of waiters, and nobody will take an order" ("Key Decisions"). We see this also as Lucille drives around the O.C. trying to find someone to unload her groceries for her, after finding out that Rosa is not "still alive" ("The One Where they Build a House").

I wish things were better for Michael, but he doesn't even recognize that the woman he inadvertently kidnaps is *not* Lupe. He sees a Mexican woman in what looks to be a service uniform, and simply assumes it's Lupe. Is he so oblivious to Lupe that he's never bothered to notice what she looks like? Does he think all Hispanics look the same? Even the best-intentioned of the Bluths, our hero Michael, falls into the trap of insisting on certain identities for those he meets.

Gob is the very definition of culturally insensitive. His notorious chicken impression (which gets him attacked in Mexico, first by the natives and later by Gene Parmesan), his repeated failure to understand the meaning of the word *hermano*, despite having taken four years of Spanish, and his insensitivity to Marta all display colossal misunderstandings of race and ethnicity.

What's philosophically and ethically interesting, however, is not simply that the Bluths operate with stereotypes. It's that the stereotypes are taken to be models for how people *must* behave. The Bluths want others to *be* their stereotypes, and they continuously attempt to make this happen. The Bluths seem hell-bent on making people live out their social identities, no matter how pure their intentions. The danger in this, of course, is that it can be stifling. We can be made to meet social expectations that we have no interest in meeting, or that make us deeply unhappy. The way others expect us to be, in other words, can actually prevent us from living a life that we regard as fulfilling. This is at the heart of the ethics of identity: because identity is a social phenomenon, it is something that can be forced on us by the world we live in. Identity, rather than expressing our values and commitments, can become another means of limiting freedom.

Stuff Whitey Isn't Ready to Hear; African-Americany Might Not Be Ready, Either . . .

No discussion of identity in *Arrested Development* would be complete without consideration of Franklin, the two-time black puppet that Gob eagerly offends others with. (Franklin is "twice black" because of a laundry accident, followed by a re-dye.)

Franklin is both a stuffed stereotype and a surprisingly edifying puppet. There's no better place to start than with the classic tune from *Franklin Comes Alive:*

> **Gob:** It ain't easy bein' white.
> **Franklin:** It ain't easy bein' brown.
> **Gob:** All this pressure to be bright.
> **Franklin:** I got children all over town.

This lovely song, a duet with Gob and Franklin, is full of error. The error is clear enough: Franklin's very voice, provided by Gob, embodies this. On one hand, Franklin is ghetto-ized; on the other hand, Gob sings about how it's difficult to live life as white. Surprisingly, besides the error of enforcing stereotypes, there's also some understanding: identities exert pressure on us, particularly when they go imperial.

Franklin is regarded as essentially black (at first, at any rate), and his activities are those stereotypical ones associated with his race. Of course, Franklin is too over the top and ridiculous for us to fail to notice that stereotypes are being employed (nobody's that oblivious!!). But the severity of the stereotypes just lets us see them all the more clearly.

> **Franklin:** Can I tell you somethin' my man?
> **Gob:** Sure, Franklin.
> **Franklin:** You are one cold [Long beep]. Speaking of mothers . . . let me give that oatmeal some brown sugar [Gob begins to make Franklin molest Lucille, as George Sr. jumps off of the couch to defend his wife] ["Meat the Veals"]

Franklin's lust for old white women isn't even his worst trait. Franklin, it turns out, is also a pimp ("Family Ties"). But despite being a sex-crazed pimp, Franklin is very sensitive to issues of race.

> **Gob:** I just had an old friend who wanted to tell you [brings Franklin around to face Lucille]
> **Franklin:** how much I miss you.
> **Lucille:** oh . . . who let this little black [BEEP] . . . [Franklin, soaked in ether, kisses Lucille, rendering her unconscious. Buster enters.]
> **Buster:** Hey, brother!
> **Franklin:** Who you callin' brother, you honky ass . . . ["Meat the Veals"]

And how could we forget Franklin's (third season) T-shirt bearing the phrase, "George Bush doesn't care about black puppets"? But despite his sensitivity to issues of race, Franklin doesn't speak for the African-American community—even if Gob sometimes acts as though he does.

Gob: Franklin said some things that whitey just wasn't ready to hear.

Michael: Gob, weren't you also mercilessly beaten outside of a club in Torrence for that act?

Gob: He also said some things that African-Americany wasn't ready to hear, either. ["Meat the Veals"]

And yet, for all the politically incorrect racial slurs, Franklin presents us with some important reminders about race. As perhaps the most imperial identity, someone's race is often wrongly regarded as telling us what we need to know about them. *Arrested Development* spoofs our tendency to let race "go imperial"—and thus also critiques the idea that race is anything essential to a person—when, in "Meat the Veals," the police confront Franklin behind the wheel of a car.

> **Cop 1 [pointing gun]:** Put your hands up or we'll take that as a sign of aggression against us!
>
> [Franklin sits silently behind the wheel of an automobile.]
>
> **Cop 2 [pointing gun, frantic]:** They're not up! He's aggressive!

Not only are the stereotypes we associate with race wrong; the very idea that race is essential to what a person *is* is wrong. *Arrested Development* manages to show this as well. Franklin, in a devastating laundry disaster, gets bleached out. In losing his color, he somehow also gains a British accent. "You've ruined the act Gob . . . ," Franklin, now bleached-white, tells a saddened Gob. The idea that the puppet's *color* made it essentially the *kind of puppet* it is also calls into question our own assumptions about race.

The philosopher Kwame Anthony Appiah (1954–) tells us that racism is not our only problem. Our bigger problem is what he calls *racialism*—the belief that races are in some deep sense *real* (in the way that stars and atoms are real).[6] Races aren't any more real than baseball teams or traffic laws: They exist only insofar as we *think* they exist. The problem with thinking races exist in the deep sense, though, is that we start thinking that people *must be* the race we identify them as. In fact, racial identity is *performed*—much as Gob performs Franklin's racial identity. It isn't something we are, but something we *do*. If we could think of race in this way, we'd make it easier to be white, and easier to be brown. (Gob: That's the exact kind of joke he would have loved. . . .)

An Ethics of Identity

Given how precarious our identities are—and how much value-baggage comes with them—we might be better off without them entirely. Of course, we all know that's not really possible. As Aristotle, Hegel, and so many others have pointed out, to be human is to be social—and part of being social involves negotiating *who* one is with who others *take one to be*. Does this mean we're as screwed as Lucille during a conjugal visit?

Maybe not. Not all of our identities are imperial ones—and maybe there's a lesson to learn there. We don't always insist that people are one way or the other. I mean, look, book reader, I don't think you are either *essentially* a Yankees fan or *essentially* a Red Sox fan. You might not be either. When you take on that identity—when you don the Yankees cap—you do so recreationally (at least I hope that's what's going on!). You can take off that identity, and no one will know any better. You won't find a box to be filled in on your job application or your health insurance about which team you like. You won't be denied a job or a proper education because of it.

The danger of identities is not that we have them, but that we tend to take them so *seriously*—and we tend to regard them as essentially who we are.[7] But, if identities are social things, we can take or leave *any* of them, no matter how *real* they are. This might well lead to a more tolerant world, where race and gender were toys to play with rather than tools of oppression.

I know, I know. I'm an idealist. A dreamer. And you're a book reader and a TV watcher. But we're more than that, too. The trick is to learn Franklin's lesson. It ain't easy bein' *anything*. The sooner we can make identity recreational, the better. Essentialized identities tend to breed hate, and hate takes a lot of time (even more than the annual Motherboy event). The sooner we give up insisting people fit our identity expectations, the sooner we'll be able to devote our lives to getting *Arrested Development* back on the air.

NOTES

1. Taylor, Charles, *Multiculturalism and 'The Politics of Recognition'* (Princeton: Princeton University Press, 1990, p. 230.

2. Ibid., p. 230.

3. Georgia Warnke, *After Identity: Rethinking Race, Sex and Gender* (New York: Cambridge University Press, 2007).

4. I borrow the term *imperial identity* from Warnke's wonderful book *After Identity*.

5. Ibid., p. 85.

6. K. Anthony Appiah and Amy Gutmann, *Color Conscious: The Political Morality of Race* (Princeton, NJ: Princeton University Press, 1996).

7. This is the line of argument advocated by Judith Butler in *Gender Trouble: Feminism and the Subversion of Identity* (New York: Routledge, 1999), as well as by Warnke in *After Identity*.

"I JUST BLUE MYSELF"

The Use and Abuse of Language in *Arrested Development*

M. E. Verrochi

The use and abuse of language is one of the most delightful features of the endlessly delightful *Arrested Development*. The show's title itself plays with at least three different senses of the phrase "arrested development": It picks out the premise of the story (George Bluth is a developer who is arrested in the pilot episode), it refers to the story line that arcs the entire series (the development of more Bluth homes is perpetually arrested), and it denotes the stunted emotional and moral maturity of the characters. But this is just scratching the surface: Much of the humor deployed in the series is the result of playing with language in one way or another.

For instance, breaking up is hard to do, but if you're an adult member of the Bluth family, it's nearly impossible (and not for the typical reasons). Picture this: In the episode "Whistler's

Mother," Gob's wife has fallen in love with the Teamocil spokesperson. The Teamocil spokesperson is Tobias Fünke. Tobias is also Gob's brother-in-law. In the following scene we see Gob's wife sit him down, in one of the brightly colored sweaters that she likes him to wear, to break the news that she is in love with someone else.

> **Gob's wife:** I'm in love with your brother-in-law.
> **Gob:** You're in love with your own brother? The one in the Army?
> **Wife:** No! I'm in love with your sister's husband.
> **Gob:** Michael? Michael!
> **Wife:** No. That's your sister's brother.
> **Gob:** No. I'm my sister's brother. You're in love with me. Me.
> **Wife:** No. I'm in love with Tobias.
> **Gob:** My brother-in-law? ["Whistler's Mother"]

Though ridiculous, Gob's interpretation, "You're in love with your own brother," is not exactly *wrong*. It is true that Gob's brother-in-law *is* his wife's brother. Likewise, when he responds, "I'm my sister's brother. You're in love with me" his interpretation of what his wife has said is somehow both correct and incorrect. Of course any native English speaker less oblivious than Gob would know that his wife was not referring to her own brother when she said "your brother-in-law" to her husband, and of course anyone less self-absorbed than Gob would assume that his wife wasn't referring to himself when she said "your sister's brother." The context clarifies what exactly is being pointed to with the use of the terms "brother-in-law" and "brother" for most of us; otherwise, her brother *is* her husband's brother-in-law and her husband *is* his sister's brother.

The idea that meaning in language cannot be divorced from the context of the utterance is nothing new. What is often overlooked, however, is the significance of the role of both the speaker *and* the hearer in speech. We know the speaker is important where meaning is concerned, and yet we often imagine that the hearer simply, passively, takes in meaning. But the role of the hearer is not simple, and certainly not passive. So much of what is funny about *Arrested Development* has to do with how the hearer interprets—or, more often, misinterprets—the context of the utterance in any given speech situation.

The problem in the previous example (for philosophers as well as for Gob) is that the term "brother-in-law" picks out multiple objects in the world (it's referentially ambiguous). But, of course, Gob's wife means something (and someone) quite specific when she utters, "I'm in love with your brother-in-law." To put a label on the confusion, we might call it the difference between *speaker meaning* and *sentence meaning*.[1] What Gob's wife "means" by what she says is that she's in love with Tobias (speaker meaning), but the meanings of the individual words of her utterance make it the case that the sentence can be taken to mean that she's in love with her own brother (sentence meaning).[2]

For a very, very, very long time, philosophers have struggled to make sense of the nuanced and vague concept that is *meaning*. Although it's safe to assume that most native, or even competent, English speakers would not interpret Gob's wife's utterances in the same way Gob does, it remains fascinating and curious that most speakers do, in fact, grasp the correct meaning of the term. How is it that most of us would (and do!) pick the "right" meaning of her utterance?

The space for humor arises in virtue of the multitude of ways that speakers and hearers can "get it wrong"—just as Gob mistakes sentence meaning for speaker meaning. The use and abuse of language in *Arrested Development* reveal interesting things about how "normal" language works (like the fact that *who is hearing a particular utterance* matters, a lot)—things we might not notice in non-comedic uses of language. *Arrested Development* pushes the application of language beyond the context in which we expect it to function—and meaning in language is all about context.

I Christen This Ship the *Lucille*

Nothing highlights the performative power of speech quite like the moment in "Fakin' It" when the kids get married. In an attempt to secure a kiss from his cousin, George Michael convinces Maeby to take part in a fake wedding for Alzheimer's patients. The first attempt is a fake ceremony that Maeby takes too literally, and she bolts. We're told that for Maeby the fake wedding was "a little too real"; the speech act of uttering "I do" with George Michael, even though the context is "playing pretend," feels wrong to her. The second attempt is "fake." Both George Michael and Maeby believe they're just role-playing. However, this time the officiant is real, and he's *not* playing. If all the right pieces come together, then the words uttered at a marriage ceremony fulfill the act of marrying. The first time around, the officiant was not authorized to marry anybody (the one presiding over the fake wedding is really a doctor pretending to be a priest and then a rabbi). The second time around, Father Ben fills in for the doctor, not knowing that it's a fake wedding. When Father Ben utters, "I now pronounce you husband and wife," he doesn't report or describe what's going on—he performs a marriage! And that's how the kids—not knowing that it isn't a fake priest—get married.

To say that speech is "performative" is to say that in certain instances, with the right people and the right context, to utter something is the same as to do something. J. L. Austin (1911–1960) was the first philosopher to extensively explore the performative dimension of speech.[3] Austin's most well-known and oft-cited example is a marriage ceremony: When you say "I do" in a marriage ceremony you do not report on the marriage but in fact get married, even if you do it based on a dare.

It's not just marriages that happen with the simple uttering of a few words in the right context with a speaker of the right authority. Suppose that I approach a yacht docked in Orange County, California, smash a bottle of champagne on its helm, and pronounce, "I christen this ship the *C-Word*." In uttering the phrase, "I christen this ship the *C-Word*," I do not report or describe the world; rather, I perform the act of christening in the very uttering of the words (as long as I have the authority to christen ships). The same goes for apologizing ("I apologize for hurting you"), promising ("I promise to meet you at the Queen Mary"), betting ("I bet ten thousand dollars on Lucille 2"), swearing ("I swear to tell the truth, the whole truth, and nothing but the truth"), and on and on.

These speech acts are *explicit performatives* in that the verb identifies the action that is accomplished (or, at least, attempted) in the uttering of the phrase. In saying "I apologize," I apologize. In saying "I promise," I promise. But the explicitness of explicit performatives isn't necessary for any given illocutionary act[4] (a performative speech act) to come off without a hitch. I can apologize by saying, "I'm sorry," or, "I didn't mean to hurt you," or, "I've made a huge mistake," and so on. I can promise by saying, "I'll be at the Queen Mary at three o'clock come hell or high water." I can bid by screaming, "10,000!" at a charity bachelorette auction. These utterances aren't explicit performatives, but they are performatives, nonetheless.[5] Actions such as promising, apologizing, marrying (whether "for real" or on a dare), daring, betting, bidding, naming, and the like can be done in speech. So can actions such as stating, asserting, claiming, arguing, protesting, affirming, and so on.

In Austin's theory of the performative nature of utterances, we find an analysis of language that acknowledges the simple fact that we *do* things with words. Such a theory implicitly recognizes that no utterance conveys meaning outside of a context; the role of the speaker, the audience, the culture, and the historical moment function as key players in understanding what a particular utterance *means*.

Austin noted that there are more subtle ways of doing something with words than constructing explicit performatives. I give you Lucille Bluth.

"I've Been a Horrible Mother."

Lucille Bluth is the matriarch of the Bluth family and (as it turns out) the master and commander of the Bluth Company. She is also one of the most quick-witted, venom-tongued characters to grace TV motherdom (perhaps ever). She quickly justifies an insult directed at a young Lindsay Bluth ("Dinner's ready! We're having *Lindsay-chops!*") as a way of preparing her for school bullying. Once when Michael suggests that Gob should be fired from the Bluth company, she assumes Michael to mean that Gob should be "gotten rid of" in the sense of "should no longer exist" (Michael: "I need you to get rid of Gob." Lucille: "That ship sailed 32 years ago."). The infinitely wise narrator confirms that no bully will ever outdo Lucille Bluth.

Words may stab *like* a knife or feel *like* a punch in the gut (just ask Buster—after being shot down by Marta, he suggests, "So that's what it's like to be punched in the face."), but they do not literally do these things. Unlike a good "Boyfights" video or a Saturday morning making cornballs, we're often wounded by words with no physical cuts or bruises to signify that harm. So how *exactly* do words wound? This is an important question for philosophers. Figuring out how words harm, as well as the way and to the extent that they do, may very well show us how to interrupt that harm. Sadly, another adage meant to help us chin-up in the face of harmful speech is also less than always true: Fighting words with words is often helpful, and can be somewhat satisfying, but not entirely so.

In "My Mother, the Car," Michael plans a surprise birth-day dinner for Lucille on two separate occasions without success. Finally, as consolation for the second surprise being a dud, Michael allows Lucille to drive them home (in spite of the fact that she's been voted the "World's Worst Driver"). As they approach a guy on the road driving a Segway in the middle of the night, Lucille, thinking the scooter driver is Gob, decides to give him "a scare." Lucille loses control of the car. The next scene opens to a chaotic mess with the car crashed, ambulance and police in attendance, and Michael in the driver's seat barely conscious. The rest of the episode is about Lucille keeping Michael hostage at her apartment, "caring" for him while he recovers from "his" bad driving accident. At the end of the episode, her children confront Lucille about her lying and manipulating. Lucille, literally and figuratively backed into a corner, cowers as she utters, "I'm a horrible mother."

Most philosophers of language and linguists alike would dub Lucille's utterance a *statement*. It's the sort of utterance that reports or describes the world (accurately, in this case). It can be true or false, and in this case, it's obviously true. J. L. Austin called such an utterance a *constative utterance* and distinguished such utterances from performatives (the kind that do what they say). Austin acknowledged, however, that the constative–performative distinction breaks down. He came to think that "stating" or "asserting" were performative verbs.[6] Stating, asserting, claiming, denying and so on are things done in language, and often accomplished simply in uttering the words, even if they don't quite fit as paradigmatic examples of explicit performatives. In this instance, however, it is clear that Lucille does more than just state something or describe herself; she performs the act of turning the table on her children simply by uttering some words. She regains control; she shifts the power back to herself and away from her children (who have gained some power as a united front against her). She fishes for a compliment. The simple statement, "I'm a horrible mother," uttered by this person to her children in this particular context, has the force of guilting her children into submission. In fact, the comedy in this scene arises when we see the result of her handiwork (the simple speech act, "I'm a horrible mother"). Success is written all over Lucille's face as her children respond in the "appropriate" way to such a speech act; they tell her she's a wonderful mother.

"Blueing" Oneself

Now consider another kind of misstep—one that revolves around the hearer, but isn't the result of mistaking sentence meaning for speaker meaning, or vice versa. When Tobias utters, "I just blue myself!" he *means* that he just covered himself in blue paint to prepare for an 8 P.M. curtain call as a (hopeful) understudy for the Blue Man Group. What he seems to imply, however, is a certain impossible sexual act. The joke is that he's oblivious to the risqué meaning of the double entendre. But the joke is possible only because meaning is often conveyed implicitly rather than explicitly. In fact, almost every comedic scene in the show involving Tobias turns on what H. P. Grice (1913–1988) called *conversational implicature*.[7] Let's consider some more examples.

Although at times filled with self-loathing and fear, Tobias never seems to lose confidence in his belief that he's an actor (or, at least, meant to be one), in spite of his inability to find and hold work (not to mention the fact that he's terrible!). His one commercial audition goes awry as he fails to realize that he's advertising a department store's "fire sale" and not merely a "fire."

In the episode "Top Banana," Tobias, yells: Oh my god. We're having a fire. . . . (*softer*) sale. Oh, the burning! It burns me! Evacuate all the schoolchildren. [. . .]

When Tobias finally calls the scene, the representative trying to cast the commercial (Lindsay's high school "best hair" counterpart, Roger Danish) pauses and then says, "Would you like to try that a little simpler, maybe?" All of us watching the show understand that Roger is suggesting to Tobias that he *ought* to try it again. But that's not what is said. Somehow we all catch on (although Tobias doesn't, unfortunately for him) that the question isn't a question at all; it's a suggestion, perhaps even a command. What Roger *means* to convey to Tobias is embedded in the utterance; the "correct" meaning is implied but not explicitly said. Philosophers call this linguistic phenomenon *conversational implicature.*

Conversational implicature arises in virtue of the fact that speech is done, more often than not, for the purpose of communicating with someone (or something) other than oneself. Language enables us to be social creatures—to engage with our environment and with others. Thus, conversation doesn't consist of a series of disconnected remarks; in fact, we would consider such an exchange irrational and weird. Rather, we move along as if compelled by some shared objective, in whatever culture we find ourselves navigating.

Grice proposes that there is some general, overarching, principle that provides the organizational structure for successful conversational exchanges. He calls it the cooperative principle (CP), and it's essentially this: "Make your conversational contribution such as is required, at the stage at which it occurs, by the accepted purpose or direction of the talk exchange in which you are engaged."[8] So, in any exchange that passes for conversation, all parties to the exchange assume at least the CP is being observed. The conversational maxims of quantity (don't over or underdo it!), quality (make it worthwhile and true!), manner (make it clear!), and relation (make it relevant!) are subcategories that indicate, with more specificity than the CP, certain organizational principles of successful conversation. Attending to these maxims will keep you in step with the cooperative principle, and attending (though not necessarily with any conscious thought to the fact that one is attending) to this assumption guides a correct reading of what's going on.[9] Thus, conversation happens smoothly and successfully.

The Bluths are masters at manipulating (though not always consciously) these conversational maxims in order to fool, deceive, or simply carry on in their own way, oblivious to anything beyond their own privileged, self-interested existence. Much of what is hilarious about *Arrested Development* comes down not to what is said *explicitly* but rather to what is implicated. Incidentally, this is precisely why the "literal doctor" jokes work out so well; in his case, when he says, for example, "[Buster] is going to be *all right*," the family (and the viewers, too) take him to mean that Buster is "alright." Of course, this is one of the only times where the Bluth family, as a whole, has to swallow some of their own linguistic medicine.

These various abuses in communication remind us that communication is context-specific, but that doesn't seem to be all they do. They also remind us how much work—most of it subconscious—goes into grasping what a speaker says on any given occasion. These instances remind us how central the role is of the hearer in smooth communication.

The Hearer Doesn't Just Lay There, Michael, If That's What You Were Thinking

The various ways language is used and abused in *Arrested Development* can shed some light on a few of the noncomedic mysteries of linguistic communication. What this series does hilariously and with consistent, spot-on skill, is exploit certain features of everyday language in order to simply make us laugh: Everything from double entendre (which happens most, if not all, of the time when Tobias speaks), polysemy[10] and homophony,[11] to utterances that implicate something meaningful rather than explicitly saying it ("I just blue myself") and speech acts that do as much as they say ("I declare this [mock trial] a mistrial"). *Arrested Development* relies for much of its humor on the power of words to *do* what they say, as well as the power of words to implicate what they don't explicitly say. In so doing, it teaches us about the role of context in grasping what is said and having what we say successfully grasped by others. *Arrested Development* shows us that it might *always* matter who is speaking as well as who is listening. Words are never uttered in a vacuum, and meaning is never understandable outside of the context of the utterance. If we ignore the multiple and various features of context, we've made a huge mistake.[12]

NOTES

1. The philosopher H. P. Grice used the terms *speaker meaning* and *sentence meaning* to delineate a very specific difference in linguistic meaning, what he also called the difference between the natural and nonnatural senses of *means*. I use these terms here more to put a name to the distinction between a speaker's intention to mean something specific with what she says and the semantic content of the sentence that she utters and less to call upon Grice's analysis of this difference.

2. Another fabulous example of comedy spawned from referential ambiguity is the multiple mistaken identities of *hermano*. At various points over several episodes in the first season (most notably "Marta Complex" and "Beef Consumme"), the word *hermano* is the crux of the story line. When Marta utters "hermano" while explaining to her mother that she's in love with Gob's brother, she means for her utterance to pick out Michael Bluth, even though the term itself can also point to (and is mistakenly taken to point to) her son's brother, the brother of the make-up artist for her show, then his brother, and so on and so forth. The term *hermano* can endlessly pick out objects in the world that fit its meaning over time, space, and location.

3. J. L. Austin, *How to Do Things with Words* (Oxford: Oxford University Press, 1962).

4. Austin distinguishes between the locutionary act, the illocutionary act, and the perlocutionary act of speech. The locutionary act is simply saying something meaningful in a language, an utterance that conforms to the correct grammar and semantics of a language. An illocutionary act is the doing of something in the saying of it, a performative speech act. The perlocutionary act is bringing about an effect in another by your speech.

5. In fact, what the act of uttering the utterance accomplishes or attempts to accomplish may be the most important dimension to such speech.

6. Ibid., pp. 121–147.

7. H. P. Grice, *Studies in the Way of Words* (Cambridge, MA: Harvard University Press, 1989).

8. Ibid., p. 26.

9. It's worth noting that a given maxim can be purposefully flouted in order to convey what we want to convey. Figurative expressions work in just this way. When George Michael's ethics teacher says she "loves" Saddam Hussein, we assume that she is purposefully exaggerating her claim in order to convey something other than love for Saddam Hussein. With attention to the context of the utterance—who is speaking, who is hearing the speech, the social and cultural location of the speech act, and so on—most of us understand the utterance as an instance of irony. The assumption is that this speaker does not *literally* love Saddam Hussein, so it must be the case that the expression is being uttered figuratively—it must be the case that she purposefully, with a wink, lies (quality) in order to convey her meaning implicitly. Of course, in the show the joke is that neither Michael nor George Michael can tell if she is purposefully flouting the maxim or not.

10. Polysemy is a term that identifies one word with multiple meanings. Consider when Buster knocks on Lucille 2's door to find her making a stew with Carl Weathers. Lucille 2 to Buster: "Hey, Buster. Gee, I thought you had class." Buster to Lucille 2: "I thought you had class." The term *class* refers the first time to attending a university course and the second time to a type of elevated personal character.

11. Homophony refers to two different words that have the same pronunciation but differ in meaning. My favorite example: "The Seaward" and the "C-Word." But an equally funny one: "Lucille" and "loose seal."

12. Special thanks to Molly, who thinks that the opportunity to write on *Arrested Development* and philosophy is at least as exciting as being the president of a "Don't Buy" company. It's really happening, isn't it?

TO BIAS TOBIAS

Gender Identity, Sexuality, and *Arrested Development*

Darci Doll

How to Solve a Problem Like Tobias

At first Tobias Fünke might simply seem clueless and socially awkward. As we learn more about him, however, his peculiarities center on questions about his gender and sexual identity. Many times throughout *Arrested Development* Tobias's sexual orientation gets called into question. Despite a variety of suggestions and implications, the answers to the questions about Tobias's sexuality are not revealed, and as a result we find ourselves analyzing his behavior in the hopes of seeing the man inside Tobias Fünke.

While figuring out just what Tobias's deal is might be important, what we can learn about gender from him is even more important. As we question Tobias's gender and sexuality, our own preconceptions come to light. These revelations help identify social presumptions, stereotypes, and biases about gender. In light of this, Tobias presents more than just a puzzle to be solved. He also presents a lesson to be learned.

A Gender Enigma

Of the many questions raised about Tobias, perhaps the most obvious is whether he's gay or straight. From the beginning of the series Tobias's sexuality is called into question. At the end of the first episode, Tobias exclaims, "What an adventure! Gang, I thought the homosexuals were pirates . . . I was waiting for the universe to provide a path . . ." Lindsay interrupts with, "You're gay." To which Tobias responds, "No, no . . . Lindsay how many times must we have this. . . ." Tobias' sexual orientation has been, and will be, an issue for quite a while.

Throughout the series we see Tobias in compromising situations and locations (how could we forget Tobias's favorite nightclub, The Queen Mary?). Then there's Tobias's penchant for unfortunate double entendres, such as this one from "Ready, Aim, Marry Me": "Unfortunately, I seem to have prematurely shot my wad on what was supposed to be a dry run, and now I'm left with something of a mess on my hands." We're perplexed by Tobias in general, and about his sexual orientation in particular. A primary cause of our confusion is that Tobias possesses and acts upon both feminine and masculine traits. Such a combination tends to raise questions about gender and sexual orientation. In the case of Tobias, we can say he's an enigma because he has an ambiguous gender.

Since Simone de Beauvoir's groundbreaking 1949 work *The Second Sex*, philosophers have drawn a distinction between sex and gender. Discussion about sex tends to involve biology— one's reproductive, chromosomal, and hormonal traits. Gender, on the other hand, involves behaviors and the attitudes we have toward them.[1] As the saying goes, sex is between the legs; gender is between the ears. Typically, the feminine gender is associated with traits such as being emotionally expressive, or relying on feelings, connections with others, avoiding conflict and (in some situations) concern with appearances. The masculine gender, on the other hand, is associated with traits such as strength, emotional composure, logical reasoning, aggressiveness (at times), and the avoidance of all things feminine.

Lots of people confuse gender and sex. They think that a male *just is* masculine, and that a female *just is* feminine. If there's anything that Tobias shows us, it's that this just isn't so. One's sex doesn't determine one's gender. I can be a very masculine female, or a very feminine male. What determines my gender is just *how I act*. What determines my sex is brute biology.

The Man Inside Him

Tobias's gender appears ambiguous for a few reasons. First, people believe (often very strongly) that men must be masculine. Tobias certainly doesn't usually exhibit the traits we'd put in the normal spectrum of masculinity, although he appears to perceive himself as masculine. In "Good Grief!" when Maeby asks Tobias whether it bothers him that Lindsay is pursuing Ice (a muscular, black man), Tobias replies, "Oh no. I am surprised, though, that she's going after someone so similar to my own type. Although I suppose we all do expose our inner desires, don't we?" He also glorifies masculine traits in the advice he dispenses. Tobias claims that self-esteem shouldn't be tied up in how you look or what others think of you, using himself as a model. In the episode "Top Banana," he states that as an actor, he faces rejection every day but that "in this business of show you have to have the heart of an angel and the hide of an elephant." Yet, Tobias, in a moment of despair over a nude shower scene, states, "Yes, I'm the doctor. The perfect husband, the big manly man. The big strong daddy." He worries that he's not living up to this image ("Marta Complex").

Despite Tobias's frequent attempts to assert his masculinity (in "Burning Love" he tells Michael he must prove himself as a "man's man"), he spends more time pursuing and acting on traditionally feminine traits and behaviors. When confronted with rejection, Tobias often excuses himself to cry in the shower (usually while huddled in the fetal position, biting on a washcloth) something often associated with the feminine.[2] Likewise, we're quick to think he's being feminine when he's knitting on the couch, engaging in crafts,[3] or dressing in women's clothes (both as Tobias and his Falidia Featherbottom persona),[4] or cooking and cleaning as Mrs. Featherbottom, or identifying himself with female actresses such as Katherine Hepburn, Jada Pinkett-Smith, and Barbra Streisand.[5] Of course, there's nothing about women that indicates a superior ability to knit, to clean, or to cook. Even associating women's clothing with the feminine shows how closely we link sex and gender. What do chromosomes have to do with knitting, or with the style of clothing I wear, or with cleaning? Nothing whatsoever.

Our confusion of sex and gender leads to our confusion about Tobias. Because Tobias fluctuates between two sets of expectations about gender and sex, we might say that his gender is ambiguous. He's biologically male, but he "acts like a girl" more often than not. We expect women, and not men, to act in a feminine way—even though we shouldn't!—and so we're confused by Tobias's behavior. We wonder what someone with a penis is doing behaving like that!

But our confusion goes even deeper. We tend to associate a man "acting like a girl" with being gay. Again, sexual orientation has nothing to do with gender. The ancient Athenians commonly engaged in same-sex relations (older men were often involved with younger boys), but they were also hypermasculine (let's kill some Spartans!). The genitals one likes one's partners to have (one's sexual orientation) have nothing to do with gender (the cultural behaviors we associate with women and men). Boy, do we make huge mistakes!

Mister Gay

Arrested Development encourages the stereotypical interpretation that there's something humorous or questionable about Tobias' gender and stresses the presumption that Tobias is gay. When Tobias says that he wants to "out that queen" referring to Ann's competition in an inner beauty pageant, Michael immediately retorts, "I think you just did," not so subtly implying that Tobias is revealing his inner nature, his homosexual identity.[6] This ties into the running gag that Tobias is not only gay, but that he's in denial about his homosexuality.[7] In "Let 'Em Eat Cake," Tobias claims to have been walking in an area (one that happens to be a gay district) that he'd never been to before, but the narrator reveals he'd been there several times before. The fact that Tobias openly denies visiting this area hints that he's hiding his homosexual proclivities from his family.

Tobias and Lindsay are rarely intimate sexually or emotionally. In "The One Where Michael Leaves," Michael finds out that Lindsay and Tobias have been sleeping in separate beds and suggests that they take the master bed once he leaves. Later in the same episode, Lindsay states that the attempt to revive their sex life was, "to be honest . . . quite awkward" (the scene cuts to Tobias practicing Kegel exercises as preparation). In the episode "Out on a Limb," when Tobias and Lindsay are intimate in Maggie Lizer's shower, the first time in the shower since the honeymoon, Tobias proudly exclaims, "and this time, no tears!" Despite these attempts, Lindsay (rather explicitly) tells her lawyer, Bob Loblaw, all of the ways Tobias has failed to satisfy her ("Forget Me Now"). Tobias's attempts to connect with her on both levels are usually amusingly awkward, lending further support to the hypothesis that Tobias is not sexually attracted to women. A case in point: In preparation for what Tobias calls "a night of heterosexual intercourse," we see a review of the last attempt, including the following awkward exchange:

> **Lindsay (affectionately):** Oh T, you're always thinking of others.
> **Tobias:** I tried that, but it didn't work, either.
> **Lindsay:** Well, maybe I would be more attracted to you if you were in better shape. You know, if you were more muscular and masculine. Does that make me shallow?
> **Tobias:** No. I was going to say the same thing to you. ["Family Ties"]

We also see suggestions of Tobias's homosexuality in his interactions with other males. Tobias thinks "everyone" is gay, and often labels other men accordingly (like George Michael, Steve Holt (!), and even one of his patients back in Boston).[8] Consider the friendship with his gym buddy, Frank, for example. In the episode "Mr. F," Frank tells Tobias he's wanted to talk to Tobias about who he is and to discuss taking the relationship to a potentially awkward level. Tobias responds, twirling his hair, "Oh well, I've been wanting to have my own awkward talk as well" (and looks down bashfully). When Frank suggests they could be more than gym buddies, Tobias exclaims, "You're blowing my mind, Frank." Yet, when Frank reveals he's an agent who would like to work with Tobias, Tobias looks disappointed and says (unconvincingly), "Oh! That is good news. I'm glad you went first." Later, in "Family Ties," when he finds a "woman" to date while in an open relationship with Lindsay, her name is Michael and she happens to be a man. While this suggests homosexuality (or bisexuality), it leaves several questions unanswered: Is Tobias really in denial about his homosexuality? Is Tobias only pretending to others that he thinks Michael is a girl? Or does Tobias really believe that Michael is a girl? The one fact that remains clear is that Tobias doesn't fit traditional gender norms.

Tobias, the Blow Hard

In addition to Tobias's behaviors and relationships, he also has the habit of speaking in double entendres. In nearly every episode, Tobias says something that can be interpreted as having not only a sexual meaning but also a specifically homosexual one. In "For British Eyes Only," Tobias visits a costume shop. The clerk (who is clearly a man in drag) says, "Look who's back. Are you going to buy this time or are you just *curious?*" Tobias replies, "I suppose I'm buy-curious. I have a big TV opportunity." Of course the clerk interprets this as Tobias's admittance to being *bi-curious* and a potential *transvestite*, and thus tells him, "This is where all the big TVs come."

The extent of Tobias's suggestive phrasing leads Michael (in "Ready, Aim, Marry Me") to encourage Tobias to record and listen to the way he speaks. Here are some of the results: "Even if it means me taking a chubbie, I will suck it up," "Oh I've been in the film business for awhile but I just can't seem to get one in the can," and "I wouldn't mind kissing that man between the cheeks, so to speak." And then there's the unforgettable "I blue myself." The fact that Tobias is apparently unaware of the double meanings of his speech is hilarious to everyone, and to some, suspicious. As a former therapist he should be aware of Freudian slips, yet he seems completely oblivious, as usual.

On occasion, Tobias's misspeaking and (alleged) naïveté puts him in compromising situations. In "Storming the Castle," when Tobias attempts to buy leather to connect with Maeby (who is wearing leather only to anger Lindsay), he asks for something that says "dad likes leather," to which the attendant replies, "Something that says 'leather daddy'?" The result of this interaction is Tobias buying S&M apparel, later finding himself at an S&M fetish club called the Gothic Asshole, rather than the Gothic *Castle* (where Gob was performing his show), and then joining the S&M themed quartet "Whips and Snaps."

Thus, while Tobias appears to be unaware of his manner of speaking, he is equally unaware of the consequences that follow from such speech. To all other parties, Tobias's double entendres are Freudian slips that tell of his ambiguous gender and sexuality. Tobias, however, is as usual unaware of the way he appears to others.

Denying the Man Inside Him

How deep is Tobias's denial? Is it actually denial, or does Tobias simply not care about our gender expectations and our compulsion to label people either "straight" or "gay"? Although the automatic assumption about Tobias's unusual habits is that he's gay, it's equally possible that he's uncomfortable with and confused by sexuality in general. The fact that Tobias is a never–nude (which is exactly what it sounds like) indicates that he's uncomfortable with his own body as well. His aversion to nudity suggests a problem with sexuality generally, and not necessarily just with women—a problem that could explain all of Tobias's "questionable" behavior.

Tobias's discomfort is clear when he attempts to explain sex to George Michael in the episode "Beef Consomme": "When a man needs to prove to a woman that he's actually {pause} when a man loves a woman and he actually wants to make love to her, something very special happens and with deep, deep concentration and great focus he's often able to achieve an erec. . . ." When George Michael interrupts, saying that's not what he was asking about, Tobias is clearly relieved and qualifies, "It was about to get a little eerrr gross."

A person who has such an aversion to sexuality would naturally be unfamiliar with sexual innuendo, turns of phrase, and double entendres. Such a person would understandably seem odd in social encounters, especially those that involve sexual suggestions. It's also entirely plausible that a person who is uncomfortable with sexuality may be genuinely uncomfortable with the traditional sexual norms. Perhaps instead of criticizing Tobias (why do we care so much about what he does with his penis?), we should look at him as a source of wisdom. We ought to ask ourselves what he can teach us about gender and gender roles. Why might Tobias be so uncomfortable with traditional norms?

Gender Empowerment

While Tobias certainly misses a lot, so do we. While we're busy laughing, we often don't realize what might be gained from Tobias's words. Tobias often uses phrases that give power to women, or the feminine generally (and remember, sex and gender aren't the same!). When talking about feats of strength, Tobias often ignores the typical references to male abilities. Instead he says things like "you'd need the strength of a she-hulk" to open a jar, as he did in "Storming the Castle."

In addition, Tobias doesn't feel bound to the traditional gendered pronouns. He uses "she" and "he" nearly interchangeably, including in his book, where he changes all pronouns to the masculine "for ease of the reader." Tobias later recognizes that perhaps it was a mistake to only focus on the masculine; he suspects that the lack of feminine pronouns may have resulted in alienation of women readers. Instead of using pronouns based on a person's sex or sexual orientation, he uses them based on behaviors and traits. Thus, he uses gendered pronouns in a way unlike the way most people tend to.

For example, when a person is exhibiting feminine traits (such as when Steve Holt (!) is cast as Beatrice), Tobias uses feminine pronouns independent of the person's biology or sexuality. Steve Holt (!) is a "she" because his *role* is that of a female. (It really is that simple, even if Michael can't see it!). Calling Steve "she" has nothing to do with sexual orientation or biology. Gender is something we *perform*, it isn't something we *are*.

Tobias is bringing challenges to the English language through gender ambiguity and novel uses of gendered pronouns. By forcing us to reexamine our presumptions about gender, he shows us that we've been wrong to assume that all females are feminine and all males are masculine (as well as the assumption that the feminine are attracted to the masculine and vice versa).[9]

Analraping Tobias

At the end of the day it's not important what gender Tobias has. Rather, what Tobias shows us is how deeply rooted *our* gender biases are. Most people quickly jump to the assumption that there's something wrong with Tobias because he falls outside of traditional gender norms. Few people, however, take the time to ask themselves why they assume that he's gay, nor do they reflect on the problems associated with making generalizations about a person on the basis of a stereotype. Additionally, people often tend to ignore why they think it *matters* whether Tobias is gay. The focus on his gender as a problem shows not only our preoccupation with gender, but also with sexual orientation. The merit of Tobias shouldn't lie in his sexual orientation—whether he's gay or straight isn't a "problem" that needs a "solution."

Moreover, focusing on biases prevents appreciation of Tobias's admirable traits. Tobias sincerely wants to be a good person. Consider, for example, the episode "In God We Trust," when he disrobes (a huge step for him!) to reveal his never-nudism because he believes it will help George Michael through his own body issues, as well as help him be a good actor. Granted, Tobias is often confused about what that being a good person entails, like when he tries to set George Michael up with Steve Holt (!) in "Bringing Up Buster," but that doesn't mean he is not earnest and sincere. He's also the type of person who focuses on capabilities, propensities, skills and interests, not restrictive gender roles. Instead of defining himself entirely in the context of what is expected of him as a man, Tobias looks instead towards the universe's plan. He need not adhere to social expectations of him on the basis of his sex and gender (many of his choices for auditions involve performances that are typically feminine, such as his excerpt from "The Vagina Monologues"); instead, he places his faith in the universe to prescribe the best course of action for him. Tobias tells the family's publicist that, "I truly believe the universe wants me to be an actor and not a doctor, I'm just waiting for a sign." And when Carl Weathers is on the same shuttle to the airport, Tobias exclaims, "Universe, You've done it again!" ("Public Relations"). Tobias believes the universe will devise a plan that's best for him based on his character and his skills, not his gender.

Tobias as the Ideal

When we stop trying to figure out Tobias's gender or sexual orientation, we can see that he has quite a bit to offer. In philosophy and different branches of feminism, androgyny has been suggested as either an ideal or an alternative to the feminine/masculine gender dichotomy.[10] An androgynous individual possesses both feminine and masculine behavioral characteristics and traits. Instead of being wholly defined by one gender, an androgynous person blurs the lines and draws from both sets of traits. The benefit of androgyny is that it removes the polarity that a gender dichotomy presents. That is, instead of being feminine *or* masculine, an individual is just a person. The focus is moved from identifying a person based on expected behaviors determined by gender, to identifying the person based on traits, abilities, and so on.

In a society with a history of oppressing one gender, gender traits often reflect (and at times reinforce) that oppression. In removing the focus on gender by focusing instead on androgyny, we can also remove some of the damage caused by past and current oppression.

Tobias might in fact be pansexual or omnisexual (much like his server gig in Reno in "The Swallows"). A pansexual or omnisexual is a person whose identity and sexual choices are not limited or determined by gender (the person may engage in sexual acts with all genders). Thus, a person who is pan- or omnisexual will have a sexually diverse personality and lifestyle and will choose sexually diverse activities with partners independent of their biology or gender. What is important about these classifications is that they remind us about sexual and gender diversity. As we encounter greater varieties of people, lifestyles, and traits, it becomes clear that the classic conceptions of gender and sexuality are no longer sufficient. In the contemporary world, we must acknowledge our past mistakes of expecting people to fit into personality types. What a person like Tobias shows us is that we needn't concern ourselves with fitting into a specific mould; we need not worry about whether we're too feminine or masculine, nor about whether our sexuality or personality conforms to "normal" standards. Instead, like Tobias, we should find the universe's plans for ourselves and follow them to the best of our abilities. Surprisingly, the problem with Tobias is that there may not be a problem at all; perhaps the problem is with social expectations about sex and gender. Perhaps we should all try to find the Tobias inside of us.

NOTES

1. Jami L. Anderson, *Race, Gender and Sexuality: Philosophical Issues of Identity and Justice* (Upper Saddle River, NJ: Prentice Hall, 2002), p. 29.

2. See season 1, episode 2, "Top Banana"; season 1, episode 3, "Bringing Up Buster"; season 2, episode 11, "Out on a Limb"; season 1, episode 11, "Public Relations"; season 2, episode 15, "Sword of Destiny."

3. In season 3, episode 11, "Faking It," we see Tobias knitting on the couch. See scrapbooking in season 3, episode 12 "Exit Strategy," and creating glitter-filled gift baskets in season 3, episode 9, "S.O.B.s."

4. In season 3, episode 12, "Exit Strategy," he's seen wearing an ill-fitting women's blazer; season 1, episode 18, "Justice Is Blind," and episode 11, "Out on a Limb," he dresses in Maggie Lizer's clothes (and in the latter, also her pregnancy suit); as Falidia Featherbottom in season 2, episodes 14–16, "The Immaculate Election," "Sword of Destiny," and "Meat the Veals."

5. See season 2, episode 11, "Out on a Limb"; season 1, episode 11, "Public Relations"; and season 2, episode 1, "Sword of Destiny."

6. The jokes about Tobias's alleged homosexuality are too many to list or summarize entirely.

7. "Out on a Limb" makes a play on this; Tobias accuses Lucille of being in denial, which he later exhibits in response to her criticism of him.

8. See, for example, "Bringing Up Buster" and "Not Without My Daughter."

9. For an additional discussion of the benefits of recreating gendered pronouns, see, for example, Leslie Feinberg's *Trans Liberation: Beyond Pink or Blue* (Boston: Beacon Press, 1999), which argues that the contemporary use of gendered pronouns puts too much emphasis on the social expectations and not enough on the humanity of an individual.

10. For example, Ann Ferguson, Mary Vetterling-Braggin, Mary Ann Warren, Andrea Dworkin, Carol Gould, Marilyn Freidman, and James Sterba, to name a few.

I'M OSCAR.COM

The Problem(s) of Personal Identity in *Arrested Development*

Kristopher Phillips

"Unfortunately for Oscar, 'you've got the wrong twin' was a common alibi" ("The Cabin Show"). Poor Oscar, nobody believes him. And why should they? Oscar looks just like George Sr., especially after George shaves Oscar's head. They're identical twins, after all. But this raises a host of important philosophical questions about the nature of personal identity—what makes Oscar *himself* and not George? What makes Oscar the same person from one moment to the next? What evidence do we have to help us tell the difference between Oscar and George?

There are a few different *kinds* of issues that philosophers raise about identity. Indeed what is often called "*the* problem of personal identity" is not one problem, but many. The first of the problems concerns what *actually* makes Oscar who he is and not somebody else (George Sr., for example). We'll call this the metaphysical question. The second problem concerns persistence: What does it take to make Oscar the same person from one moment to the next? And the third problem concerns evidence: How do we *know* who is who? As we'll see, *Arrested Development* teaches us the most about the first kind of problem, but it also offers some insights into the problems of persistence and evidence.

Bland (I mean, Ann), Marta, the Richters, Aristotle, and the Metaphysical Question

As we all know, Michael is no fan of his son's girlfriend, Ann. Ann is *essentially* a bore. She and her family hold their parties on Bethlehem time and engage in hours upon hours of silent prayer. Ann is not the most beautiful woman in the world, nor is she ugly . . . she's just *bland*. In fact, Ann was played by two different actresses, and the transition from one to the next was nearly seamless. I guess that's what happens when your most defining feature is that you lack any defining features (I mean, under her school picture, it said "not pictured"). But Ann is not alone in her replaceability; indeed she is not the only character who was played by multiple actresses. Marta, Gob's on again, off again girlfriend, is herself portrayed by a pair of actresses. Michael, though, is a big fan of Marta. Marta is *essentially* everything that Michael could want in a woman (for himself or for his son): She's attractive, family oriented, charming, and successful. Despite the fundamental differences between Marta and Ann, both characters are seamlessly played by two different actresses. How could this work out so well? In answer to this question, we can appeal to the philosophical and scientific works of Aristotle (384–322 BCE).

According to Aristotle, each species has some specifically defining feature or set of features that make it what it is rather than some other species.[1] He famously held that a "[hu]man is a rational animal." This was what Aristotle took to be the *essential characteristic* that belongs to all and only humans. This isn't to say that all humans are *essentially* and totally the same, for that's obviously false. Rather, Aristotle says that all humans share this characteristic, and this explains why they're all so similar, as well as what's unique about them. (Aristotle also defines the human being as a featherless biped—but this doesn't capture what's *unique* about human beings). If something lacks the unique characteristic that makes us different from the other featherless bipeds (namely *rationality*), then it's not a human.

But this alone doesn't explain how two women could so easily be one character. Yes, both women are featherless bipeds, and both have the rational capacity Aristotle argues is unique to human beings. But these similarities don't explain the differences between individuals that belong to any particular group. To account for these differences, Aristotle argues that each individual person has different kinds of characteristics, some *essential* (necessary), and some *accidental* (contingent). This is the key to understanding Aristotle's view on what makes Annabelle (I only call her that because she's shaped . . . she's the belle of the ball!) who she is and not somebody else. Essential properties are those that Ann cannot get rid of *and still be Ann*. Ann, it seems, could change her hair color, or could have had different colored eyes and it wouldn't mean that she's literally a *different* person. Buster lost a hand to a seal, but he didn't cease being Buster, even if he did become "a monster" (or "half-machine"). As we saw, Ann can even ditch her religious beliefs and take up a relationship with Gob, and still be Ann. These are all *accidental properties*. If Ann ceased to "have a low center of gravity, [so that] you can't knock her down" or ceased being bland, then, it might seem that we're not talking about the same person anymore.

Similar things can be said about Marta. She seems to be *essentially* beautiful, charming, an accomplished actress, and, well, Hispanic.[2] These are the traits common across the two actresses who portray her. Her height, her hairstyle, and so on, aren't things that the two Marta's have in common, but that doesn't really seem to matter much. These aren't *essential* to who Marta is. The *essential* traits we're considering are all fairly shallow, though. We don't know much about Marta, and as central a character as Ann is, we don't know all that much about her, either.

Many of these *essential* traits have to do with the way Ann and Marta appear. But what if, as is the case with George and Oscar, the people we're wondering about look as if they are (and actually *are*) qualitatively identical? This is exactly the case with Andy Richter and his four identical siblings, who appear in "S.O.B.s." The only way to distinguish between these five characters (Andy, Rocky, Donny, Chareth, and Emmitt) is by appealing to what the infinitely wise Narrator offers as the defining characteristic of each of them, "there's Andy, the show-off; Chareth, the flirt; Rocky, the stuntman; Donny, the sensitive one; and Emmitt, but we're not allowed to show his face . . ." This way of explaining the essence of each person may at first glance appear to be a promising answer to the metaphysical question, and maybe even the evidential question. After all, if an Andy Richter look-alike charges into your house and pretends to slam you against a wall and hold you there, you can probably assume that it's Rocky (as long as he leaves you in total control of the situation). Yet, this might not be as promising for the evidential approach as it first appears. Andy himself shows up at the "Save Our Bluths" banquet pretending to be Emmitt, and, though suspicious, nobody can prove it is really Andy. So, maybe this speaks against essences as a solution to the evidential problem.

The case of George and Oscar isn't so different from that of the Richters. George and Oscar have very different essential properties. Oscar isn't particularly ambitious, while George is overly ambitious. Oscar isn't worried about money, while that's all George seems to value. These essential differences aren't enough to convince the cops, but they are enough for Michael. When Oscar states, "I understand, your child comes first," this cues Michael in to Oscar's identity ("The Cabin Show").

Despite the seeming promise of the essentialist approach to the metaphysical question, our discussion of *the essence* of a person is still pretty mysterious. What *is* this essence that we keep talking about? So far we've enumerated a few different things that might be *examples* of an essence, or of an *essential property*, but we're still a far cry from knowing just what the essence *is*. So let's consider how Aristotle's view could be revised to make it more informative.

Oh My God . . . You're Oscar. Dot com. [and George Sr. and the Metaphysical and Persistence Problems]

Aristotle's work in philosophy and science was hugely influential for a long time after his death (in 322 BCE). Many medieval theologians and philosophers, such as Augustine of Hippo[3] (354–430) and Thomas Aquinas (1225–1274), constructed philosophical systems at least in part based on Aristotle's principles. During this period, there was an "exapting" of the idea of the essence from Aristotelian doctrine, to the Christian doctrine of the immaterial soul (the bearer of mind and personality, and the part of humans that survives the death of the material body).

This approach was picked up by the first modern philosopher, René Descartes (1596–1650), who was a devout (and some argue, terrible) Catholic. Descartes made *substance dualism* one of the cornerstones of his philosophical system. Substance dualism is the view that there are two distinct kinds of stuff that exist, matter or body and mind or spirit, and neither one requires the other to exist. According to Descartes, each of us has our own immaterial soul, and that soul is the bearer of our individual mind; it makes us who we are. In a way, the soul *is* the essence of a person. In light of other traditional theological considerations, the "essence as soul" approach becomes a bit less mysterious, and a bit more robust. This gives us a more straightforward answer to the metaphysical question: What makes George Sr. different from Oscar? Oscar has a unique soul, and thus we can explain the fundamentally different feel that Oscar's character has from his brother throughout the show. George and Oscar have different immaterial souls, despite having such similar bodies.

Aristotle thought that a person consisted of a specific combination of essence (he called it "form") and matter. Ann is bland and is bound to her bell-shaped-body, Marta is a fox, and is bound to the material that makes up her body. The Cartesian (Descartes's) view,[4] on the other hand, isn't committed to this at all. There's nothing specific to your body that's essential to you on his view. To be sure, Oscar and George have different bodies, Oscar has hair (oh, that hair . . .) while George doesn't. They can stand next to each other, and that would only be possible if they had numerically distinct bodies. To be sure, there's a fair amount of switching places because their bodies look so much alike. On Descartes's view, if George had the power, he could switch souls with Oscar, and that would probably solve many of his problems. By doing this, he wouldn't have to rely on the Cornballer's shoddy craftsmanship to burn off Oscar's fingerprints, or his adopted Korean child, Annyong (hello!), playing Uncle Sam in a school play so that he can "take wig"; he could *really* switch bodies.

This raises an interesting question about the interaction of the soul with the body: if George and Oscar did switch souls, would the George body, now inhabited by Oscar's soul, start growing hair? Just how the soul interacts, and is joined with the body is an issue central to the philosophy of mind, and most philosophers after Descartes find his explanation wanting. But that's an issue for another day. Descartes, of course, doesn't think that any of us have the power to swap souls with one another (and isn't really concerned with George Sr.'s lack of hair) and, if he's right, that's a good thing for Oscar. It's hard enough for him to stay out of prison as it is.

Aside from the obvious explanatory value of the Cartesian picture for the metaphysical question (which seems to speak in favor of the Cartesian picture), Descartes's use of the immaterial soul provides an answer to the persistence problem. Descartes maintained, in accord with the Judeo-Christian tradition, that the soul can and does survive the death of the body. This offers an easy answer to the persistence problem: If the soul is what makes George different from Oscar, and George's soul will survive the *actual* death of his body, as opposed to the less-than-perfect deception attempted by the Mexican authorities, then it seems to follow that from one moment to the next, George's soul does the work of making him continue to be George Sr. But, as with most answers to philosophical questions, the Cartesian view is not without problems.

Larry (the Surrogate), Forget-Me-Nows, and Locke's Criticism of Descartes

John Locke (1632–1704) is not just a character from *Lost*. There was also a John Locke who was a contemporary of Descartes, and on more than one occasion took on Descartes's views directly. In his *Essay Concerning Human Understanding* Locke not only considers the Cartesian view on personal identity, but he offers a troubling counterexample. The idea is basically this: if Descartes is right that the soul makes you, *you*, then what if Socrates's soul "revolved around several human bodies" and what if we met a man who was able to convince you that "his had been the *soul* of Socrates . . . would any one say that he, being not conscious of Socrates' actions or thoughts could be the same person as Socrates?"[5]

This is a simple question, but it gets to the heart of Locke's objection, and it foreshadows his own account of personal identity. Before we get to what Locke thought makes you *you*, we should flesh out this objection a bit. It's a strong objection that hits the Cartesian view on two levels. First, it's a metaphysical objection. If the soul is immaterial (does not exist in space, time, and so on), then we may end up having to say that you are *the same person* as many people that have lived before you. This is a startling conclusion, and when we consider how bad we feel for Oscar as he sits in prison, wrongly accused of his brother's crimes, this might make us uncomfortable. If Oscar has the soul of many others from the past, and the soul makes him who he is, then he *may well* be responsible for having done something terrible in the past (albeit distinct from the terrible things George Sr. has done). If this is right, we shouldn't feel so bad about Oscar's time in prison, even if he doesn't remember doing any of those terrible things *he* did.

The second way that this objection hits the Cartesian account is related to the first; it is an evidential objection. Even if Oscar does share a soul with another person from the past, he has no way of knowing this fact. Locke even takes it a step farther, suggesting that, for all we know, we may well have, over the course of our lives, dozens of souls being swapped out. What seems constant, and what seems to be good evidence for our identity isn't an ethereal soul that, by definition cannot be experienced, but rather the continuity of our memory (or mental states more broadly construed, as contemporary philosophers have argued). Doesn't it seem, Locke suggests, a flimsy basis for identity to say that what makes us who we are, and who we are over time, is something that we can't experience, like a soul?

Think of George Sr.'s surrogate, Larry Middleton. He was hired by Bob Loblaw to be George's eyes and ears when meetings were going on outside of the penthouse where George was under house arrest. During one of these meetings, it becomes clear that somebody (namely, Tobias, or "Mr. F") has tipped off the Bluth Company's investors that the family hasn't yet begun construction on their next phase of development, resulting in the investors coming to inspect the land. Gob comes up with a plan to try to fool the investors by building a model town (complete with a model train) just outside the window of the Bluth model home. Larry inadvertently ends up being controlled by Buster, and notably nothing about Larry's external appearance changes, nothing about his verbal delivery changes, and nothing about his mind changes, despite the drastic "internal" change in control from George to Buster. What changes is who's in control of Larry. Most of the time it's George Sr., but when he gets stuck in the wall trying to find a way to escape his house arrest, Buster takes over and manages to fool Gob into thinking that it's still his father in control. In this case, what is changing could be construed as analogous to souls being swapped out. It is important to note here that Larry's mind survives the switch of souls. Larry's mind operates just as it did under George Sr., and as the Narrator says, "only Larry was disappointed, but he was such a pro, you'd never know it" when he (controlled by Buster) and Gob begin building their "tiny town." The episode ("Mr. F") continues, and the deception is nearly perfect. Gob, Lucille, and everyone else see Larry *as* George Sr. Of course, he's not George, nor is he Buster, he's Larry, but we don't know anything about him, other than that he's some "stupid parrot man with a camera in his hat" who nicely illustrates Locke's objection to Descartes.

The very nature of the soul is that it's not something we can experience, either from the inside or the outside. Thus, Locke's objection works on two levels, and Larry illustrates both nicely. But he also exhibits Locke's own account of personal identity in much the same way. We already noted that Locke's objection functions, at least partly, on the evidential level. Locke was primarily worried about how we could *know* that we have one and only one soul, and that it is specific to us.

He was also concerned to point out that our experience of identity is consistent with having infinitely many souls over the course of our lives. As such, he wanted to focus on how we experience our uniqueness, and our persistence over time. As we have noted, Larry, himself, did not experience a change in his own mind when the "soul" that was underlying his experiences changed. He was still unhappy about having to spend time with Gob, as we might all be, despite what he was obliged to say and do. We certainly wouldn't want to say that *Larry* became a different person when he was controlled by different people, but, it might be said, this is required on the Cartesian account of personal identity—at least as far as the analogy goes. But, what might we say if Larry were to lose his memory? Well, this hasn't happened to Larry, but there are others in the show to whom it has happened.

It's no secret that Gob maintains a ready supply of "forget-me-nows" (roofies). What might Locke say about the "temporary forgettiness" that, for example, Rita feels when Gob feeds her a roofie? If Gob's audience members learn how a trick is done, or if Buster happens to club a lady-friend of Michael's, or worse yet, Gob happens across George Sr. and Lucille becoming intimate in a marital trailer, you can bet that Gob will do anything he can to wipe their (or his) memory clean. But in what sense, then, can we say that the *same* person saw or knew these things? Locke has this to say, "to punish [George Sr.] waking for what sleeping [George] thought, and waking [George] was never conscious of, would be no more right, than to punish one twin for what his brother-twin did, whereof he knew nothing, because their outsides were so like that they could not be distinguished . . ."[6]

So Locke suggests that the very reasons that we must reject the Cartesian picture imply a more plausible account—one where identity is determined not by the physically essential features or by some immaterial and inexperienced soul but, rather, by a connectedness of memory. Oscar cannot be held responsible for the actions of his "brother-twin," because he had no knowledge or memory of doing those things. Oscar didn't do them. Similarly, George can't be held responsible for selling marijuana in Mexico, since his "brother-twin," you know, "brothero," had all the memories of doing that, and George didn't. Gob even recoils in horror at the suggestion that he had seen his parents becoming intimate—"What is wrong with you!? I did no such thing!" This seems to imply that Gob is, himself, a Lockean about personal identity. *He* didn't see his parents. He has no memory of it, so it must've been somebody else.

Locke's memory criterion, as philosophers call it, offers us an answer to the evidential problem of personal identity, and offers an intuitive answer to the persistence problem, but doesn't give us as much by way of a metaphysical explanation as the Cartesian picture does. Still, many philosophers find such an approach immediately appealing. True to form, however, as a philosophical position it has its problems—problems that can be illustrated by way of Gob's commitment to this view.

Thomas Reid, Gob, and the Problem of the "Forget-Me-Now"

Thomas Reid (1710–1796) thought that Locke had made a number of mistakes in his assessment of what makes us who we are. Reid thought that the evidential problem of personal identity often results in a confusion—specifically, we confuse the *evidence* that we have for the belief that we are who we are (and that we exist over time) for what *actually makes us* who we are (and are over time).[7] This is an important point, but it may not be the most important objection that Reid lodged against Locke's memory criterion.

Reid's most famous objection can be paraphrased in the following way: Imagine an aged Gob, looking back on his life. No doubt he'll want to write a memoir about his life, taking himself far more seriously than he should, and despite the fact that it *should* be called "huge mistakes" it'll probably not include any mention of such events ("I've never admitted to a mistake . . . what would I have made a mistake about?").

As he looks back on his life in preparation for writing his masterpiece, he remembers the time that he released a seal into the wild after giving it the taste for mammal blood. By Locke's criterion, this makes the aged Gob the same person as the middle-aged-seal-watching Gob, because they share a memory of this event. At the time that Gob heard about Buster's hand, he remembered from his childhood one of the elaborate lessons that George Sr. had orchestrated using a one-armed man (J. Walter Weatherman). This makes the middle-aged-seal-watching Gob the same person, by Locke's memory criterion, as the child, lesson-learning Gob.

But, so the story might go, a lifetime of taking roofies in order to wipe his memory free of having seen his parents becoming intimate, or to forget bonding with his son, has caused some serious damage to the aged Gob's brain, and as a result, the aged Gob doesn't remember that elaborate J. Walter Weatherman lesson. By Locke's criterion then, the aged Gob is not the same person as the child Gob. Reid points out that identity is a transitive relationship (if x is equal to y, and y is equal to z, then it simply must be the case that x is equal to z), and, in light of this logical truth, we have a problem for Locke's conception of personal identity. Old Gob is identical to middle-aged Gob, and middle-aged Gob is identical to young Gob, and so (by the transitivity of identity), old Gob must be identical to young Gob. But since old Gob does not remember what young Gob did, they cannot be the same person. Since Locke is committed to holding that old Gob both is and is not identical to young Gob, we have a serious problem. This seems especially bad for Gob, since he at least tacitly endorses Locke's view—Gob is now committed to believing that he *both* is and is not himself, and while this would not be the only time he's held obviously false or problematic beliefs, *we* don't want to be forced to believe crazy things like this.

Some philosophers have learned a lesson from Gob, and developed more nuanced variations of Locke's criterion in an attempt to provide answers to the problems Reid raised for Locke, and by association Gob. But Lockean attempts aren't the only game in town. A revised essentialism is seeing an increase in popularity in some philosophical circles (though it does look quite different from Aristotle's essentialism).

Even though we haven't resolved the problems of personal identity, I think that we've learned a lot about the problems facing us around every turn. As Michael would say, "that's enough family stuff for today."

NOTES

1. Aristotle, *Metaphysics* Z 3–4.

2. Such characterizations of essences can be dangerous though. For a more full exposition of how dangerous essentialism can be, see Chapter 8, "What Whitey Isn't Ready to Hear."

3. Strictly speaking, Augustine was more heavily influenced by Plato (Aristotle's teacher), but for our purposes, this is fair enough, as Augustine was hugely influential on Descartes, whom we'll consider momentarily. And, to the best of my knowledge, Augustine had nothing to do with hippopotamuses.

4. We call Descartes' view *Cartesian* because of the name Descartes used (Cartesius) for his writings in Latin.

5. Locke, *An Enquiry Concerning Human Understanding* (EHU), vol. II (New York: Dover Press, 1959), Chap. 27, p. 455.

6. Ibid., p. 460.

7. Thomas Reid, "Of Mr. Locke's Account of Our Personal Identity," in *Essays on the Intellectual Powers of Man*, first published 1785.

PART FOUR

THE ONE WHERE THEY DO EPISTEMOLOGY

YOU CAN'T DO MAGIC

Gob Bluth and the Illusionists' Craft

Michael Cholbi

"Magic is the simplest kind of primal escape form. We take Mother Nature and turn it upside down, to be able to dream about something that doesn't really exist."

—(David Copperfield)[1]

"I've made a huge mistake."

—(Gob Bluth)

The Bluths are a vocationally challenged bunch. Indeed, not a single member of the extended Bluth clan enjoys legitimate, continuous, satisfying employment. But would-be illusionist Gob Bluth is perhaps the most vocationally challenged of them all. Gob destroys the (often live) props used in his act (seeking a refund for a dove that he smothered in his jacket,

"Top banana"); forms a "Magician's Alliance" to protect illusionists' secrets, only to inadvertently disclose such a secret (first in the "Pilot" and again in "Storming the Castle"); horrifies children with his botched illusions (causing a bloody wound in his neck, "Storming the Castle"); and patches over his ineptitude with cheap theatrics, including his signature reliance on the '80s power-pop anthem "Final Countdown." Indeed, his one apparent success as an illusionist—making the Bluth family yacht disappear—turns out not to be an illusion at all. (He simply sinks the yacht.) But despite this apparent incompetence, Gob insists that he's a consummate professional.

> **Michael Bluth:** So this is the magic trick, huh?
> **Gob:** Illusion, Michael. A trick is something a whore does for money. ["Pilot"]

Career Advice from Aristotle

That Gob so clearly wants to be a competent illusionist, but so routinely fails at his chosen profession, raises the question: Why does he fail? Perhaps surprisingly, this is a question that philosophy, and more particularly, ethics (the branch of philosophy concerned with how to live) can help us answer. Philosophers have long been interested in why some human beings excel at what they do whereas others fail. For example, Aristotle (384–322 BCE) argued that many activities, including the activities characteristic of different professions, realize their purpose when those activities produce the goods associated with them. For instance, the activity of medicine, when done well, results in healthy patients. Hence, doctors, who are supposed to be experts in the activity of medicine, do their jobs well when the treatments they prescribe make their patients healthier. The same philosophy holds for every other professional activity. A professional succeeds at her chosen profession when she produces the good results the profession aims at. A successful teacher makes her students more knowledgeable; a successful architect or developer designs buildings that are attractive, durable, and functional (unlike the Bluth Company homes); a successful airplane pilot delivers passengers to their destinations promptly, safely, and comfortably; and so on.

Aristotle's account of how people excel in various activities implies that there are three explanations of why people fail at their chosen professions. The first is that a person may not appreciate the aims of her profession. For instance, a doctor who thought that the aim of medicine is to entertain his patients with wisecracks would be seriously confused about what medicine is *for*. This doesn't mean that cracking jokes has *no* place in the medical profession. Rather, a doctor who thought that making jokes, instead of making people healthier, was the aim of medicine would have the wrong professional priorities and would probably make for a poor doctor. Comedy is his calling.

But there's no evidence that Gob misunderstands the aims of his profession. If anything, Gob understands all too well that an illusionist is an entertainer, and the competent illusionist entertains her audience by surprising, delighting, or puzzling them. So Gob doesn't fail as an illusionist because he fails to appreciate the aims of that profession.

Aristotle's account offers a second possible explanation for Gob's failure: Some people simply don't care about the aims of their chosen profession. Many people fail at their professions, often becoming jaded and unhappy, because they're not strongly committed to the profession's aims. A successful doctor must actually care about, and be motivated by, improving people's health; a successful teacher must actually care about, and be motivated by, students' learning; and so on. A professional who never cares about the profession's aim, or one who cares for a while but suffers midcareer "burnout," will not be motivated enough to produce the good results associated with the profession.

But this won't explain Gob's failed career as an illusionist. If anything, Gob shows extraordinary motivation to continue his career, despite a long record of failure. No matter the setback, Gob ends up back on stage, dagger in his mouth, attempting to saw people in half or make a yacht disappear. He's got both the appreciation of and the desire to realize the aims of an illusionist.

The Virtues of an Illusionist

Aristotle has a third explanation of professional incompetence. Some people lack the appropriate traits or knowledge needed to succeed in a profession. Aristotle refers to the traits or knowledge required to excel in a profession as "crafts," and each profession has not only its own distinctive aim or result but also a body of knowledge, methods, or traits through which that aim or result is produced.

A successful doctor, for instance, has to know the workings of the human body, as well as the likely effects of different drugs, surgeries, or other treatments. (The lack of this knowledge explains why Michael's surgeon, Dr. Frank Stein, has so many "little whoopsies," like leaving his snippers in Michael's abdomen in "Sword of Destiny.") A doctor also has to know a variety of investigative and diagnostic methods (checking a patient's pulse, examining a patient's throat, ordering a CAT scan, and so on) and when to use these. And a successful physician also must have certain traits of character: compassion, attention to detail, judicious judgment, a welcoming but authoritative presence, and strong communication skills (not exactly a strong suit for the all-too-literal Dr. "I'm sorry to say this, but it's too late for me to do anything for your son" Fishman). Without these traits, a doctor will not make people healthier, no matter how committed she is or how fully she appreciates this aim.

So what kinds of knowledge or traits are necessary to succeed as an illusionist? Magicians and illusionists are entertainers, but they entertain their audiences in a very specific way. Audiences are delighted and intrigued by illusions because, when they're taken at face value at least, illusions are impossible events. Handkerchiefs cannot turn into doves. A person cannot be sawed in half, survive, and then be joined together again. In prescientific times, audiences likely thought that illusionists actually were conjuring up magic, channeling demonic or supernatural powers. Modern audiences, on the other hand, are curious and puzzled by illusions, but understand the illusion as the product of the entertainer's technical ability (her "sleight of hand"). They are deceived by the illusion, but also intrigued to understand how that deception occurs.[2]

What does it take for aspiring Gobs to be, unlike Gob himself, *competent* illusionists? Modern illusionists are not conjurers, but methodical, diligent, scientifically oriented engineers of human experience. The task of creating an illusion is one of *reverse engineering*, usually involving the conceptualization of the illusion (what the audience is supposed to believe they saw) followed by the development of the techniques through which the illusion will be accomplished. Complex illusions, such as David Copperfield's making the Statue of Liberty disappear, are the product of trial and error overseen by teams of expert craftsmen, including the performer. Such illusions can require many years of preparation and hundreds of thousands of dollars of equipment and overhead costs. Moreover, just as in scientific experimentation, illusionists must perfect their illusions through repeated practice, modifying and refining illusions until the desired effect is achieved. The modern illusionist must, therefore, be *dogged* and *diligent*.

On top of that, an illusionist needs a wide range of *technical knowhow*. The illusionist's ability to create a sense of bafflement or surprise in her audience depends first on her knowing how to manipulate the objects used in her act—be they playing cards, rabbits, silk scarves, or the sword of destiny—so as to give the audience the impression that she's done the impossible. So it's not just the kinesthetic ability to move these objects in the desired ways; it's also the knowledge of how manipulating these objects produces beliefs in the audience—beliefs that what was witnessed couldn't have actually happened. A successful illusion requires the complex understanding of how, by seeing stage objects in motion, observers will be led to believe they perceived something impossible. This is why illusionists deploy a variety of dramatic techniques—distraction, building tension, and so on—that psychologically prime the audience to experience the sense of illusion. Of course, the illusionist understands how the impossible was made to seem possible, but the audience does not. For the illusionist, there's no illusion going on. As the science fiction writer Robert Heinlein put it, "One man's 'magic' is another man's engineering."[3]

Lastly, magic is a profession that thrives on *humility*. Being a magician is surprisingly challenging work, and an illusionist is no more successful than her illusions. She cannot simply will herself to success. Ultimately, an illusionist must respect the limits set by the laws of nature and by the audiences' expectations of what they perceive. For it is only by knowing these limits that she can create illusions that seem to transcend them. Tricks fail, props don't work, the audience can see through the ruse. A person without humility, someone who cannot be humbled by the labor and insight needed to make illusions succeed, is not cut out for this profession.

Why Gob Can't Do Magic

Doggedness, diligence, technical knowhow, knowledge of human psychology, and humility: Doubtless there are other traits or skills a successful illusionist needs, but these are central to her success. What is crystal clear is that Gob Bluth is sorely lacking in all of these virtues, and actually has the corresponding vices in abundance.

Let's start with those two D-words, doggedness and diligence. Loath though he would be to admit it, Gob Bluth is a slacker. Aristotle once remarked, "What we learn to do, we learn by doing."[4] But Gob hardly appears to prepare for or practice his performances at all, and what preparation he does is ridiculous (painting a Q and a diamond on his chest and asking his nephew to pick a playing card from a deck in the hope that it will be a queen of diamonds). He is seemingly unable to learn from his mistakes, and his inattention to detail is staggering. In "The Cabin Show," he misreads a letter from "S.A.D." (a company that reunites long-lost fathers and sons) as a letter inviting Gob to reunite with George Sr., when in fact it was an attempt by Gob's illegitimate son, Steve Holt (!), to reunite with Gob. As for technical knowhow, Gob cannot operate a trapdoor or keep a dove alive long enough to use it in his act. In the episode "Public Relations," Gob gives the elderly volunteer (for his illusion, the Aztec Tomb, err, box, we'll just say "box"), the founder of the prestigious Milford School, last-minute instructions about a "hidden panel" inside a coffin, only to end up "killing" him. Gob aspires to grand illusions, but struggles to perform simple sleights of hand that can be mastered by anyone with a library card (or a connection to the Internet) willing to practice them. His struggles are captured on a "Girls with Low Self-Esteem" video, where Gob repeatedly fails at basic tricks.

But of all Gob's shortcomings, his lack of humility is most responsible for his failed magic career. Hardly an episode passes where we're not reminded of Gob's perpetually low self-esteem and his parents' indifference to him. In a classic case of overcompensation, Gob appears to deal with this poor self-image by fancying himself a heroic and misunderstood genius, ready to serve as the president of the Bluth Company, fool a polygraph, or break into the Orange County prison using a jetpack, all in vain efforts to win his father's love. In the eyes of modern psychiatry, Gob exhibits symptoms of bipolar disorder, alternating between depressive phases (feeling despondent and worthless) and manic phases (feeling elated and highly confident, as if he is on a mission). Whenever Gob's self-image is punctured, he breaks down, sometimes being pushed over the edge, as when he attempts to hang himself for making a fool of himself in front of the prosecutor, or when he swallows a "forget-me-now" to cloud his memory of having bonded with his illegitimate son. We see both the fragility of Gob's confidence and his need to compensate for low self-esteem in this memorable exchange with his brother Michael, who is ever eager to puncture Gob's inflated self-image:

> **Gob:** It's a classic bait and switch. This is a decoy cooler. We take it in, switch it with the one from the photo, and get out of there. Kitty comes back, everything's normal. It's like we were never there.
> **Michael:** But Dad's gone.
> **Gob:** Long gone. But it buys us all the time in the world. I got it back, Mikey, the self-confidence. I am a magician.
> **Michael:** No, I'm saying, when Kitty comes back and notices that Dad's gone, the first thing she's going to do is check the cooler to see if the evidence is there. It buys us, like, one second.
> **Gob:** I'm a worthless magician. ["Spring Breakout"]

But it's the manic phases that seem to influence Gob's behavior more and that derail his magic career. Not only does Gob lack humility; he has its opposite, the excessive and tragic pride Aristotle called *hubris*. This lack of humility can be played for laughs precisely because Gob himself is blithely unaware of both his incompetence and his lack of humility. Gob's failures are not only professional, of course. Other human beings and their motivations are opaque to him. But his ultimate failure is that he is not self-critical in the least, and as a result, he is opaque to himself.

Inscribed above the Temple of Apollo at the ancient Greek site of Delphi is one of the best bits of advice ever offered: "Know thyself." Gob is an abysmal failure when it comes to following this advice. His lack of self-knowledge explains his inability to learn from his mistakes and may also go a long way in explaining his misguided hope that a singular event—making the family yacht disappear, or attempting to bury himself in his father's coffin, only to emerge alive a week later ("Good Grief!")—will be his salvation, or will at least get him the cover of *Poof* magazine. Sadly, Gob does not recognize his own impotence, a common tendency among incompetent people.[5] Thus, the only illusion Gob consistently succeeds at creating is an illusion about his own competence.

Gob not only lacks the professional virtues of a magician; he exhibits full-out contempt for professionalism of any kind. Gob's various professional shortcomings—a misguided faith in his own abilities, rashness, a lack of professional diligence, elaborate scheming and showmanship substituting for talent—are all evident in his greatest professional flop, the "Sword of Destiny" trick. Seeking to impress the more famous magician Tony Wonder, Gob plans an illusion in which he is to be stabbed in the belly with a sword. Showing his typical impulsiveness, he buys an ancient Chinese sword—the real deal, not a trick sword—from a shady storefront healer. Having been banned from the Magician's Alliance, Gob persuades his brother Buster to pretend to be the head illusionist while Gob serves as his assistant. But Gob ends up slicing off his brother's artificial hand, thrilling the audience and impressing Tony Wonder enough that he offers to have the pair on his next DVD. Though feebly protesting "It's not the real illusion!" Gob concludes that appearing on the "DVD is the destiny the sword has chosen" for him, and in a meeting with Tony Wonder, Gob reveals that he, not Buster, is the real illusionist and will be performing the *real* "Sword of Destiny" trick in a subsequent performance. In the course of that performance, Gob's own fingers are sliced, only to be reattached later in a purposely botched surgery.

Impulsive bravado, an unflappable belief that he is fated to greatness, the substitution of theatrics for careful preparation, an intense yearning to belong to a professional community, a nearly lethal level of carelessness: The "Sword of Destiny" is Gob's magic career in a nutshell.

The Magical World of Gob

Aristotle's account of professional excellence helps us pinpoint the source of Gob's failed career. Gob appreciates the aims of his profession and holds those aims in high esteem. He clearly sees magic as his calling, but he's the antithesis of the competent modern illusionist. Vain, lazy, gullible, and prone to foolish dreams, he stands in stark contrast to the modest, hardworking, skeptical, and self-critical illusionist. On one hand, a competent magician has a decidedly unmagical worldview. Gob, on the other hand, embodies the magical worldview, and it is this worldview that makes professional success so elusive for him. In Gob's eyes, success in magic comes not from mastering a sophisticated scientifically informed craft but from an elusive, mystical quality of heart that he believes he has. In "Missing Kitty," George Michael briefly serves as Gob's assistant. He later dismisses George Michael, saying "You don't have the magic in you," pointing to George Michael's heart. "You never did. You don't have it here."

But "having it in here" isn't enough. In "Top Banana," Gob's brother Michael asks Gob to mail a letter so that Gob will feel important and included in the family business. In an "act of defiance," Gob attempts to throw the letter into the ocean, only to have the wind repeatedly blow it back in his face. Could there be a more pathetic image of Gob as a failed illusionist, vainly but persistently trying to "take Mother Nature and turn it upside down?"

Of all of Gob's "huge mistakes," opting for a magic career may thus be the most ironic. As Aristotle helps us to see, Gob's professional failings are ultimately failings of *character*. He fails not because of bad luck or external circumstances, but because of durable features of his personality—laziness, inattention to detail, lack of humility, and so on—that show up most markedly in his professional efforts. Gob simply does not have the traits or attitudes required for success as a magician—or, arguably, for any profession.

NOTES

1. Robin Leach, "David Copperfield Finds the Fountain of Youth," Vegas Pop, posted February 21, 2007, http://www.vegaspopular.com/2007/02/21/david-copper field-found-the-fountain-of-youth-photos-exclusive/.

2. James Randi, *Conjuring* (New York: St. Martin's Press, 1993), and Jim Steinmeyer, *Hiding the Elephant: How Magicians Invented the Impossible and Learned to Disappear* (New York: Carroll and Graf, 2003).

3. *Glory Road*, (1963).

4. *Nicomachean Ethics*, Book III, Chapter 1, 1103a32.

5. Gob is a prime example of the "Dunning-Kruger effect," wherein individuals who are incompetent wildly overestimate their competence and cannot recognize competence in other people either. The classic article describing this effect is Justin Kruger and David Dunning, "Unskilled and unaware of it: How difficulties in recognizing one's own incompetence lead to inflated self-assessments," *Journal of Personality and Social Psychology* 77 (1999): 1121–1134.

IS JUSTIFIED TRUE
BLUTH BELIEF
KNOWLEDGE?

Brett Coppenger and Kristopher Phillips

The Bluths know lots of things. George Michael knows that he loves his cousin Maeby. Gob and the members of The Magician's Alliance know the secrets that explain their tricks.[1] Buster knows a great deal about agrarian business in the eighteenth century, but doesn't know whether or not we should be concerned about an uprising. And if you were to ask Michael whether or not he was dreaming (or more likely, having a nightmare), he would sadly, but adamantly, maintain that he knew he was awake and that his experiences were all real.

Epistemologists (philosophers interested in figuring out what knowledge is) have attempted to find the necessary (required) and jointly sufficient conditions (those conditions that together are enough) for knowledge. By examining the previous examples of Bluth knowledge, we can illustrate the necessary and sufficient conditions of the "traditional account" of knowledge.

I Didn't Even Know That There Was a Cabin . . . He Wasn't Taking Me To . . .

For starters, George Michael, Gob, Buster, and Michael all believe something—of course, they don't all believe the *same* thing. George Michael believes that he loves his cousin, Gob has all kinds of beliefs about how magic tricks are performed, even if he's not very good at performing them himself, and so on. So belief is necessary (required) in order to have knowledge. But is belief enough? If you believe something, does that mean you know it?

Consider Tobias's belief that he is an exceptional actor. Tobias is utterly convinced that he's first-rate artiste (not to mention that he was a first-rate analrapist), despite his utter failure at landing any sort of role as an actor. Perhaps we can place some of the blame on Carl Weathers, but epistemologists are not in the business of finding out who is at fault, we're worried about *knowledge*!

The problem with Tobias's belief is that it's unjustified. Tobias believes that he's a great actor, but he holds this belief despite a preponderance of counter-evidence. It's hard to imagine why Tobias thinks he can act. Mere belief, while necessary for knowledge, is not sufficient—we need something more. A belief must be *justified* if it's to count as knowledge. A paradigm case of unjustified belief might be a belief based on a magic eight ball. If, for instance, Lindsay came to believe that she was not a Bluth simply because she asked a Magic Eight Ball "Am I a Bluth?" and the Magic Eight Ball responded, "All signs point to no," we would still say the belief is unjustified, even if it turns out to be true.

Surely though, if someone believes something and they are justified, then they would know it, right? Maybe not; consider

Michael's automobile accident from the episode "My Mother the Car." After regaining consciousness, Michael came to believe that he'd tried to hit his brother Gob with his father's car. Michael is justified in his belief, since his mother told him that he was responsible and his injuries were consistent with his mother's explanation of what happened. But, does Michael *know* he tried to hit his brother with the car?

Once again, there's still something missing. The problem with Michael's belief is not that it failed to be justified, but instead, that the belief turned out to be false. Lucille misled Michael into thinking he was at fault, when in fact she had intended to run down her first born, and then with her superhuman strength switched places with Michael. Of course, earlier that day, Michael had witnessed his mother struggling with the weight of some "groceries," further suggesting to Michael that what actually happened was impossible. We all know, though, that the "groceries" were actually gold bars disguised as protein bars—in an attempt to help prevent George Sr. from being strangled in the shower . . . or worse, but let's get back to Michael.

Clearly then, not only must one have a belief and have justification for that belief, but the belief must also be *true*. And with this we've finally arrived at the traditional account of knowledge where knowledge is defined in terms of justified-true-belief (we'll call it JTB). On this account, JTB is necessary and sufficient for knowledge; if someone knows something, it follows that her belief is justified and true. If someone has a belief that is justified and true, then she has knowledge.

With the traditional account in mind, let's return to our original examples. If George Michael knows that he loves his cousin Maeby, then he must not only believe it, but also have justification for believing it (in this case all he needs is awareness of his own emotions). And, of course, his belief must also be true. Similarly, to say that Buster knows a great deal about agrarian business in the eighteenth century is to say that

Buster has beliefs about eighteenth-century agrarian business (something having to do with how best to avoid an uprising perhaps?), that those beliefs are justified (Buster's extensive academic background would likely provide him with the relevant sort of justification), and that his beliefs were true.

The traditional account seems to achieve our goal, but in recent decades it has met with serious scrutiny and almost universal rejection.

As You May or May Not Know [JTB] and I Have Hit a Bit of a Rough Patch . . .

Just as we used examples to show that mere belief (Tobias's acting) or justified belief (Michael's accident) are not sufficient for knowledge, the philosopher Edmund Gettier developed famous examples that are intended to show that JTB is *itself* not sufficient for knowledge. If Gettier is right, then the traditional account of knowledge would fail to provide necessary and jointly sufficient conditions for knowledge. The following two cases come from Gettier himself:[2]

Case 1: Best Man for the Gob . . . I mean, Job!
(1) I am justified in believing that Jones will get the job, and I am justified in believing that Jones has ten coins in his pocket.
(2) On the basis of (1) I deduce that the man with ten coins in his pocket will get the job.
(3) It turns out, unbeknownst to me, that I have ten coins in my pocket and I will get the job.

Case 2: Headed down old South-America Way, eh Brown?
(4) I am justified in believing that Jones owns a Ford.
(5) On the basis of (4) I deduce that either Jones owns a Ford, or Brown is in Barcelona.
(6) It turns out, unbeknownst to me, that Brown is in Barcelona.

In each of these Gettier cases it is granted that there is a justified belief, (1) and (4), respectively. It is then shown that the justified-belief can be used to entail (have as a required consequence) another claim, (2) and (5), respectively. The difficulty comes when we realize that we can have a justified-*false*-belief, which entails some other belief, and by sheer chance, the other belief turns out to be true; as with (3) and (6). Gettier concludes that, in both Case 1 and Case 2, we would have JTB but not knowledge.

While both of these Gettier cases rely on an explicit inference from one premise to another, philosophers have created Gettier-*style* cases so that there seems to be no inferential step at all.[3] Consider another famous Gettier *style* case from Alvin Goldman:[4]

Case 3: It's not a Real House, Mom . . . That's All right, He's not a Real Man.
(7) I am justified in my belief that the thing I am pointing at is a very nice barn.
(8) Unbeknownst to me, I am driving in Fake-Barn-County, where one in every four barns is real and the rest are barn-façades.
(9) As it turns out, the thing I am pointing at is a barn [and in fact, a very nice one].

In what *must* have been an attempt to maintain relevance in the philosophical literature, the writers of *Arrested Development* incorporated Gettier-style cases into the show. Consider the following three examples:

Case 4: Faith is not a fact!
In an effort to make the most of his time in prison, George Sr. makes a collection of divinely inspired videos called *Caged Wisdom*. Under the guise of an ardent fan of his Torah teachings, an undercover government agent, Cindi Lightballoon, is able to get close to George Sr. Before

long, Cindi develops an infatuation with George Sr., and in order to show her love, Cindi discloses to George Sr. that the government has no case against him. As a result, George Sr. forms the belief that "we need to fight this thing, the government has no case against me . . . I know this for a *fact*." George Sr.'s belief seems to be justified. After all, he heard directly from a government agent that the government has no case against him. Additionally, it is true that the government doesn't have a case against him. However, unbeknownst to George Sr., Cindi only believed that the government had no case against him as a result of blind faith (thanks to a failure on Cindi's part to discern *Caged Wisdom* from the *Caged Wisdom* "Blooper Reel"). But surely, we would not think George Sr. actually knew the government had no case, even though it was a justified true belief. Contrary to his suggestion, George Sr. did *not* know, for a fact, that he could "beat this thing."

Case 5: Hey, Uncle-Father Dad

Late one night, in the midst of a deep sleep (likely after being tucked in by his mother), Buster is suddenly woken up by a person who he takes to be his Uncle Oscar. After all, the person is visually identical to his Uncle Oscar, long hair and all. The brief conversation between Buster and his visitor consisted of the visitor telling Buster a number of things including, notably, "I'm not your uncle, I'm your father." As a result of this interaction, Buster forms the belief that "my uncle is my father." Surely Buster's belief is justified, someone who looks exactly like his uncle tells him that he is his father. Additionally, it *is* true that Oscar is Buster's biological father. However, unbeknownst to Buster, the person who woke him up was George Sr., cleverly disguised as his twin brother Oscar. As a result, we would not want to say that Buster *knows* that Oscar is his real father, even though it was a justified-true-belief.

Case 6: She's a lawyer! That's Latin for 'Liar'!

After running into an old fling, Maggie Lizer, Michael comes to believe that Maggie is not carrying his child. After all, he knows Maggie as a pathological liar. So when she eventually tells him that he *is* the father of her child, he has reason to disbelieve. Additionally, Michael enlists Tobias and Lindsay to search Maggie's house for evidence. Lindsay calls Michael to tell him that they discovered a pregnancy bodysuit in Maggie's possession. Thus, Michael's belief that Maggie is not carrying his child seems to be justified. It also turns out that Michael's belief is true: Maggie is not carrying his child. This is a particularly tricky case, because for a moment it seems as though, unbeknownst to Michael, the pregnancy bodysuit that Tobias and Lindsay found really belonged to one of Maggie's clients. Thus, it seems extremely lucky that Michael formed the belief he did. Of course, that suit really did belong to Maggie all along, but Maggie replaced it with a more realistic, synthetic model. As a result of all of this, we would not want to say Michael had knowledge, even though he had a justified true belief.

First You Dump All Over It, Now You Want to Know How It's [Solved] . . .

While many epistemologists have been skeptical of the original Gettier cases, the success of the *Arrested Development* Gettier-*style* cases forces additional refinement to the traditional account of knowledge. Although there is, in general, agreement amongst contemporary epistemologists about the failure of the traditional account of knowledge to offer necessary and sufficient conditions for knowledge in light of the Gettier problem, it would be a stretch to say that there is much, if any, agreement about how best to solve the problem.

With this lack of consensus in mind, we can characterize three different approaches to resolving the Gettier problem.

First, we might reject the project of offering an analysis of knowledge altogether, and by doing so dissolve the motivation for considering Gettier-*style* cases. Second, we might refine how justification is understood so that Gettier-*style* cases are blocked. Third, we might try to find a fourth condition that, when taken along with JTB, provides what we're looking for in an analysis of knowledge.

Philosophers who adopt the first approach argue that Gettier-*style* cases show us that the project of analyzing knowledge in terms of necessary and sufficient conditions was doomed from the start.[5] We might even argue that every epistemologist is committed to taking some epistemic concept as unanalyzable, and perhaps there are reasons for us to think that knowledge should play that role. Of course, such a view is at odds with many of our intuitions about what knowledge is. After all, it seemed obvious that at the start of this chapter we could take belief to be a necessary constituent of knowledge. If we can get one constituent that seems to be obviously required for knowledge, then it would be awfully weird if, in reality, we couldn't offer any analysis.

Perhaps, then, we should reconsider what these Gettier-*style* cases taught us. Maybe, the problem is that our notion of justification needs refinement. We can go about this in a number of ways. One proposed solution to the Gettier problem is to raise the degree of justification required for knowledge. On this view, the justification required for knowledge is certainty (or evidence that implies the impossibility that the belief is false). As a result, Gettier-*style* cases are avoided because knowledge requires certainty, and each of the Gettier cases seems to rely on the possibility of false belief, where the belief just happens to be true. Yet, such an answer to the Gettier problem would have devastating consequences when it comes to the *extent* of our knowledge. Surely, there are many things we know, but aren't certain of. Indeed most of the examples that we took at the outset of this chapter

(George Michael's love for Maeby, Buster's extensive and use-less academic "knowledge") would fail if this were the require-ment. Alternatively, Bertrand Russell (1872–1970) suggested that we maintain fallible justification, but require that knowl-edge cannot come by way of false premises.[6] On such a view JTB is necessary and sufficient for knowledge, but a belief is only justified if it is not inferred by a faulty line of reasoning. On this type of view, the Gettier cases fail to be counterex-amples since they involve the bad kind of inferences. Such a solution, however, requires locating the illicit inference in Gettier—and that's no easy task.

Finally, one might proceed by trying to locate a fourth con-dition necessary for knowledge. Proponents of this view also differ wildly in what they take to be the fourth condition, and a survey of such views would be far beyond what we care to do here. However, we can briefly consider one type of approach, where the necessary addition to JTB is that the belief in ques-tion be caused in the right kind of way.[7] Thus, it could be argued that in the Gettier cases, the belief fails to be knowledge because it was not caused in the right kind of way. In effect, the belief only turned out to be true due to sheer luck, and not because of an appropriate belief-forming process. Clearly though, this approach requires an adequate analysis of "appropriate belief-forming processes," which is far from easy. Finally, solutions of this sort take as necessary for knowledge something external to the knower. As a result, such a view is at odds with much of the history of epistemology. After all, don't we want to know when we have knowledge?

Despite the difficulties involved with each approach, we are left with the intuition that in many cases we do have knowl-edge. In fact, even people like the Bluths often know things, yet clearly the project of figuring out just what knowledge is, and what kinds of things can be known, is still far from done. If only the series had not been canceled, maybe these issues could have finally been resolved.

NOTES

1. Of course by "trick" I mean "illusion," since a trick is something a whore does for money . . . or cocaine!

2. Edmund Gettier, "Is Justified True Belief Knowledge?" *Analysis* 23 (1963), pp. 121–123.

3. In fact, there is a debate about whether there can be Gettier-style examples that do not involve any inference. Although this might not seem important, the crux of some responses to the Gettier problem relies on the existence of an inference.

4. This case is a paraphrased version of the Gettier-style case that appears in Alvin Goldman, "Discrimination and Perceptual Knowledge," *The Journal of Philosophy* 73 (1976), pp. 771–791.

5. For a defense of this type of approach, see Timothy Williamson, *Knowledge and its Limits* (Oxford: Oxford University Press, 2000).

6. For what could be interpreted as an approach of this type, see Bertrand Russell, *The Problems of Philosophy* (Oxford: Oxford University Press, 1959).

7. For a view of this type, see Alvin Goldman, "A Causal Theory of Knowing," *The Journal of Philosophy* 64 (1967), pp. 357–372.

BUNKERS AND BALLS

Arrested Development,
Underdetermination, and the
Theory-ladenness of Observation

Michael Da Silva

Choosing Between Wayne Jarvis
and Barry Zuckerkorn

In the first season of *Arrested Development*, the Bluth family is forced to continue using Barry Zuckerkorn as their lawyer, much to Michael's consternation. Michael would rather have the highly professional services of Wayne Jarvis, who ultimately instead prosecutes the case against George Sr. But in at least one area Jarvis doesn't measure up to Zuckerkorn. Jarvis doesn't know balls.

Wayne Jarvis: Michael, this is a close-up satellite photograph of the Iraqi countryside. See this little series of hills around that stream? Those are bunkers. We believe those bunkers contain weapons of mass destruction. We also believe that your father was building on that land to hide them.

The Bluth family fears, and Wayne Jarvis is certain, that George Sr. helped hide the weapons by building bunkers. The U.S. government agrees and begins to mobilize troops, including Buster Bluth, to escalate the war in Iraq. It's only at the end of the episode that the family's ambiguously homosexual (bisexual?) lawyer, Barry Zuckerkorn, rightly points out that the landscapes in the photographs are actually testicles.

Wayne Jarvis: Michael, when we started talking to you, we didn't have anything. But now . . . we got something. And you're going to do time for it.
Barry Zuckerkorn: Those are the pictures? Those are balls . . . This close they always look like landscapes. Those are balls.

Thus, the episode "Sad Sack" raises the question: Do we see only what we expect to see?

Following the work of Pierre Duhem (1861–1916) and W.V.O. Quine (1908–2000), many philosophers in the twentieth century accepted that theories "underdetermine" facts, or that there are rival and competing views on what a given image may be or what a given piece of data may mean. No theory can exclude its rivals by appeal to the world alone. The problem is that there are lots of different ways to describe the world, all of which are compatible with what we see *in* the world. In the bunker-balls photo, for example, there's nothing in the photograph itself to tell a viewer whether he or she is looking at bunkers in Iraq or an analrapist's testicles.

Rather than test a theory against data, people often use the theory to explain the data. Philosophers call this the "theory-ladenness of observation": The very theories we advocate can *determine* what we see. What one imagines or sees is constrained by the dominant theory one is working with. In our day-to-day lives, we accept theoretical commitments and these commitments affect how we interpret the world around us. If one expects to see balls, one will see balls; if one expects to see bunkers, one will see bunkers.

The theory one chooses is thus very important. If one accepts the theory, for instance, that George Sr. helped hide weapons of mass destruction in Iraq and thus sees bunkers in the photograph, then war follows. This is a significant result of the theory-ladenness of observation for policy procedures. For an unprepared soldier like Buster Bluth, it could have disastrous consequences.

Wayne Jarvis's desire to do his job and convict George Sr. colors Jarvis's interpretation of what he's looking at. Zuckerkorn's interpretation, too, reflects his own deep interests. Fortunately, the narrator knows all. He solves the debate by coming in as the "voice of God" and clearing things up, telling us, "Tobias had inadvertently photographed himself while learning to use his camera phone" (cut to scene of Tobias in the bathtub with Gob's phone). The viewer, then, has enough information to decide between two competing theories.

As much as we like Ron Howard telling us what's what on *Arrested Development*, we don't have the benefit of an omniscient narrator in everyday life. How do we choose? How *can* we choose a theory? How do we know whether we're looking at bunkers or balls?

The Lenses of Wayne Jarvis, Barry Zuckerkorn, and George Michael Bluth

In *The Structure of Scientific Revolutions*, American philosopher of science Thomas Kuhn (1922–1996), a follower of the Duhem-Quine thesis, suggests that we all see things through the lens of the dominant theory (or paradigm) in society. We live our day-to-day lives as if the dominant theory *did* fully determine the facts of the matter. Our observations, then, are theory-laden. Scientific revolutions occur when our paradigms fall into crisis—when we want to answer questions our paradigms make it difficult to even *pose*.

The theory that George Sr. is a criminal and conspired with Saddam Hussein is dominant at the time that the photographs are discovered. Bluth is a known criminal, has escaped prisons in two different countries, and has been seen with Hussein by the time the "bunker" photographs are found. It doesn't take a lot of imagination for Wayne Jarvis to accuse George Sr. of the "medium to heavy treason" that the photographs apparently prove. It's also not too difficult to understand how the key seats of knowledge, such as the government and media, can accept Jarvis's suggestion. When there is no agreement on what the dominant theory about a given topic should be, however, the foundation of the dominant theory erodes. Barry Zuckerkorn's new theory on what the photographs could be showing created a crisis, which (in this case quickly) necessitated the selection of a new dominant theory. It also raised new questions that couldn't be asked before, like, "Whose balls are these anyway?" and, "Why would someone take a picture of his balls?"

Not all crises, however, are so easily resolved. George Michael's inability to pass the eye exam in "Sad Sack" makes this clear. While George Michael is not explicitly testing out new theories, he is literally testing out new lenses through which to see the world. He's unable to find one that allows him to see things clearly. Thus, when Maeby asks George Michael if he has seen her mother, George Michael is only able to commit to a "seems possible." In the absence of the right lens through which to see the world, or an objective criterion for picking the right lenses, George Michael is stuck in a skeptical moment: he knows not what he sees. It's only when he abandons his glasses that he's able to say he's seen the now infamous image on the cover of the magazine before. He's seen Tobias's testicles as Tobias clumsily climbed to the top bunk of the bed they share. But George Michael still can't take on the role of a privileged observer, helping to solve the theory crisis. He doesn't say where he saw the balls in question. He just says, "I've seen this before."

Thus far, there are no set criteria for choosing between competing theories in a moment of crisis. Without the right theoretical lens through which to see the world, we're stuck in a skeptical moment. We're left wondering how to choose between competing theories. Kuhn's answer is that our theory choices are largely determined by social and political factors, not by appeals to truth. Who we are and where we've been matters a great deal when it comes to choosing between theories. In the absence of clear criteria for choosing between competing theories, we often rely on social and political concerns to make a choice. In this case, the government's desire to convict George Sr. (and, perhaps, the Bush administration's desire to invade Iraq and defeat Saddam Hussein) makes Jarvis's theory easy to accept.

But Jarvis's theory doesn't get to the truth of the matter. Jarvis's theoretical commitments lead him to see bunkers that just aren't there. Political concerns lead to accepting the wrong view in this case. Of course, Kuhn would point out that calling the interpretation wrong *already* depends on a scientific paradigm. Paradigms are inescapable—but that doesn't mean every paradigm is as good as every other. If we don't want to mistake balls for bunkers, or to be led erroneously to war, the Zuckerkorn paradigm is a pretty darn good one.

Q: War! What Is It Good For?!
A: Well, Certainly Not Buster Bluth

Kuhn has often been charged with epistemic relativism, the faulty doctrine that knowledge is relative to (or determined by) one's culture. When accompanied by a belief that no culture is superior to any other, a relativistic position can reduce conversation to a "Who's to say?" argument. There are neither facts of the matter, nor superior theories. There are only local truths. But, as we've seen, some theories have better results than others, though determining which results are better will obviously depend on what we're interested in, be it going to war, appreciating testicles, or something else.

While choosing Jarvis's theory may have positive political consequences for the Bush administration, which can use the photographs to justify invading Iraq, it has a negative political impact on Buster Bluth, who must either fail his military training or be mobilized long before he's ready. Given Buster's inability to hold down any job or perform any tasks not designed for a specialist at a university (or arcade), it's unlikely that he'd survive the war. Moreover, many other young Americans would surely die. Even though Jarvis's theory is defeated, Buster still takes a punch from his motivational coach, Gob, as a result of his perceived need to climb a wall in order to finish military training before the new mobilization date. Letting the powerful people in a paradigm determine the limits of knowledge can have undesirable consequences, to say the least.

Kuhn denies that there are "facts of the matter" that allow us to choose theories, but he doesn't hold an "all theories are created equal" view in *The Structure of Scientific Revolutions*. Rather, Kuhn uses an evolutionary metaphor to describe different criteria for determining when a dominant theory rules. According to Charles Darwin, the species that survive are those whose random mutations are best suited to their environment. And according to Kuhn, the theories that survive are those best suited to solve the problems they establish: "Later scientific theories are better than earlier ones for solving problems in the often quite different environments to which they are applied."[1] But solving problems isn't the same as moving closer to a theory that explains everything. It's part of the nature of scientific theories to have anomalies (things that can't be explained). Nevertheless, some paradigms are better at answering certain questions than others, even if we can't say that they're a "better representation of what nature is really like."[2] Kuhn doesn't believe in ultimate Truth. He thinks the question of which theories better represent what's "really there" in nature is impossible to answer.[3]

Does the narrator in "Sad Sack" refute Kuhn's claim that there's no ultimate truth? Has Ron Howard, the brilliant actor, producer, and director managed to refute one of the greatest philosopher's of science of the twentieth century? The Lord God Opie tells us that Tobias took a photograph of himself in the bathtub—and we *see* it. Is this trouble for Kuhn?

Not really. Kuhn acknowledges that we can determine (in retrospect) which theory is better suited to answering questions that interested and perplexed scientists at a particular time. We can determine which theory is better, in retrospect, when the epistemic crisis is solved and the military crisis is averted; even fighter pilots are able to confidently assert that they were "looking at balls."

But if our paradigms determine what we can see, where do crises come from? As we've seen, *all* paradigms have anomalies. These are usually just dismissed (science will figure it out eventually, c'mon!), but every once in a great while, resolving the anomaly becomes all important. In this sense, it's a good thing Barry is there to challenge Jarvis. "Those are balls!" is a challenge to a whole dominant regime. Barry's sexual experimentation and consequent familiarity with how male genitals look "close up" helps us get outside of our theory-laden perspective.

How to Choose Between Bunkers and Balls

The "Sad Sack" scenario shows us how important it is to be able to decide between competing theories. To avoid the feedback loop in which the theory determines what one sees, and what one sees determines whether there is a problem with a theory, there must be something outside of a theory to determine whether it's worth adopting or not.

Kuhn, in fact, recognized the necessity of external criteria for choosing a theory. In "Objectivity, Value Judgment, and Theory Choice," Kuhn outlines "five standard criteria for evaluating the adequacy of a theory" and says that he agrees "entirely with the traditional view that they play a vital role when scientists choose between an established theory and an upstart competitor."[4] Kuhn's five criteria are accuracy, consistency, scope, simplicity, and fruitfulness. As the word *standard* implies, these are hardly novel criteria, leading many of Kuhn's critics to accuse him of turning away from what made his position interesting in the first place. Nevertheless, there is intuitive appeal to these criteria, and it's worth considering whether the Jarvis Theory of Iraqi Thunder (JTIT) or the Zuckerkorn Testicular Closeup Theory (ZTCP) better meets these criteria.

Accuracy is mostly a predictive criterion; the theory that better predicts occurrences is the better theory. When we're concerned with something that has already happened, like the bunker-ball quandary, this concept of accuracy isn't a useful criterion. A more useful concept of accuracy, but one that Kuhn neglects, is based on correspondence. Which theory better matches the world? Where Barry has seen testicles and George Michael has seen Tobias's testicles, ZTCP is the more accurate theory. To this day, no one has seen WMDs in Iraq. Both theories are internally consistent, but only ZTCP is consistent with things that we know to exist in the world. JTIT posits a previously unseen entity, the Iraqi WMD bunker, which is inconsistent with what we know exists in the world. On the other hand, the criterion of fruitfulness is defined by the ability to produce new phenomena for research. So the discovery of WMDs would make JTIT the more fruitful theory.

Without that discovery, though, both theories only account for one phenomenon, the existence of a photograph. Zuckerkorn's theory has the advantage of being far simpler. "This close they always look like landscapes," is a far simpler description than Jarvis's multiple-sentence theory. And that's not only because Zuckerkorn is a master of word economy who once summed up a whole plea by saying "it's very long" (of course, the fact that he hadn't read that plea helped). By contrast, the length of and variables in JTIT, tempts one to compare it to a conspiracy theory.

It's difficult to pick a winner in many of the categories. If, for example, one values fruitfulness above all, the JTIT looks attractive. The government's desire to find WMDs, for instance, would make them apt to accept his theory. Kuhn certainly realizes that it will be rare that one theory wins in every category and that the victories may be slim. He also recognizes that some people will value some criteria over others. He is not, however, willing to rank the criteria or make a more complex metric of theory choice. At the end of the day, one just needs to know he or she is "looking at balls."

Who Knows What Balls Look Like?

Having established some basic ground rules for how to tell whether you are looking at something through the right theoretical lenses and thus *what* we know, it is worth exploring *who* actually knows what they're looking at. Who we accept as knowing about things—who we accept as a privileged knower—is an important question. Scientists, lawyers and, yes, even philosophers often fill this role. TV critics are supposed to know what is worth watching, but we may privilege critics as knowers and still not listen to them. TV audiences failed to listen to TV critics' supposed sage opinions about the necessity of watching our beloved *Arrested Development*, for example.

Wayne Jarvis is a government lawyer and this makes him a privileged knower, able to mobilize the U.S. government and military in short order. Barry Zuckerkorn's role as a lawyer should make him a privileged knower, but his incompetence and idiocy undermine his position. Just think of his unfamiliarity with the plea bargain and his failure to remove the dingdong from its foil wrapper prior to microwaving it. In "Sad Sack," though, Zuckerkorn's sexual proclivities make him a privileged knower. The show frequently teases Zuckerkorn for his sexual experimentation. In "Justice Is Blind," for instance, when Michael suggests that the plea is so long that Barry was right not to read it and that they should just take it, Barry responds, "I could kiss you on the nuts." And in "Motherboy XXX," Zuckerkorn talks about catching a judge at a drag club. Gob then asks him what he was doing there. It's his familiarity with male genitalia that makes Zuckerkorn the privileged knower in this scenario, just as his role as a lawyer would make him a privileged knower in most scenarios (if he were a competent lawyer)

Of course, if it were enough to know a pair of testicles to become a privileged knower of photographs of testicles, then George Michael could have been the hero. Even though George Michael may recognize the image in the photograph, he doesn't offer a theory that explains it. Indeed, George Michael is the opposite of a privileged knower in "Sad Sack." Wearing prescription glasses that he doesn't need, George Michael is stuck in a skeptical moment where he cannot assume any knowledge. In one of a few episodes where he has privileged knowledge, he's unable to articulate even the most basic statement of facts. One's epistemic position, then, is a social position. Knowing things isn't enough to make you a knower. Zuckerkorn may be the one who recognizes the balls and creates the theory, but it takes numerous government agencies to accept the theory and the mass media to proliferate it. Zuckerkorn alone, then, is not recognized as a knower until his knowledge is corroborated and disseminated. In *Arrested Development*, knowledge is societal and political.

In the Absence of Opie (Sorry, Ron)

I've referred to *Arrested Development*'s narrator "Opie," a reference to Ron Howard's childhood role as Opie Taylor on *The Andy Griffith Show*. Likewise, Barry Zuckerkorn's jumping a shark recalls his earlier role as the Fonz on *Happy Days*. The humor in Barry's jumping the shark relies on the viewer being familiar with the actor Henry Winkler's previous roles and the actions of his character on a decades-old sitcom. The theory-ladenness of observation, then, is important not only for policy and psychology, but is embedded in the very fabric of *Arrested Development*. One cannot see the deeper layers of humor in the show unless one is a certain type of person, the type of popular culture junkie who would research the show's characters and actors to understand its many allusions. There is, then, a dominant theory at work that defines even our sense of humor.

Unfortunately, we don't always have a narrator like Opie to clear up our theoretical confusions, or even to give us the proper background knowledge to understand what we're looking at (if only!). In the absence of a narrator to tell us how to choose between competing theories, we need some guidance. To save Buster Bluth from going to "Army," one needs to be able to tell whether one is looking at bunkers or balls. Kuhn's criteria are a good starting point. Like the creators of *Arrested Development*, Kuhn highlights the social and political aspects of knowledge in keeping both with the Duhem-Quine thesis and with the needs of a maladjusted mother's boy who has been signed up for the military against his will. Choosing to believe Barry Zuckerkorn may have negative consequences for Tobias's psyche. But the public display of the analrapist's genitalia never would have taken place had Wayne Jarvis recognized the theory-laden nature of his own observations and stopped to think about what he was really looking at. And that might be the central lesson here: Sometimes it's hard to know balls when you see them.

NOTES

1. Thomas Kuhn, *The Structure of Scientific Revolutions* (Chicago: UP Chicago, 1996), p. 206.

2. Ibid., p. 206.

3. Ibid., p. 206

4. Thomas Kuhn, "Objectivity, Value Judgment, and Theory Choice," in M. Curd and J. A. Cover (eds.), *Philosophy of Science: The Central Issues* (New York: W.W. Norton and Company, 1998), p. 103.

PART FIVE

SOLID AS IRAQ: POLITICS AND ETHICS ARRESTED

NO TOUCHING!
GEORGE SR.'S
BRUSH WITH TREASON

Douglas Paletta and Paul Franco

George Bluth Sr. is a bad man. Just look at the evidence: George Sr. made his own children fight each other for his profitable video series *Boyfights*, he cheated on his wife every Friday for years with his secretary Kitty, and, after the United States banned his frying contraption the Cornballer, he marketed it in Mexico despite the very real risk it posed of burning off one's fingerprints. In addition to this impressive (but far from exhaustive) list of moral failings, George Sr. just may be a traitor against his country. He admits as much in the episode "Visiting Ours," telling his son Michael that he's currently in prison because there's a "slight possibility" that he may have committed some *"light* treason." The nature of George Sr.'s (possible and lightly) treasonous act remains secret until local newscaster Trisha Thoon's hard-hitting report on Saddam Hussein's mini-palaces in Iraq. Not only were these palaces clearly American built, but Michael quickly realizes that the mini-palaces eerily resemble Bluth model homes in both appearance and shoddy workmanship.

Thus, it comes to light that George Sr.'s alleged treason consists in building mini-palaces for Saddam Hussein, America's enemy at the time. In doing so, he violated the sanctions against doing business with the so-called rogue regime. Even worse, those mini-palaces may have served as hiding places for weapons of mass destruction, which prosecuting attorney Wayne Jarvis points out potentially upgrades George Sr.'s crime from light to *medium or heavy* treason.

Now, there's very little question that George Sr. violated the laws of his country by building mini-palaces in Iraq for Saddam, no matter how shoddily constructed or how poorly the fixtures stayed together. Moreover, George Sr.'s actions, including running from his arraignment after hearing the list of charges against him read all at once, seem to indicate that he recognized the seriousness of his crimes. But, what is it about his actions that made them treasonous? If they were in fact treasonous, does it make sense to call that treason "light" or "medium to heavy"? And on what basis would it make sense to call treason light: because he was a patsy of some shadowy British syndicate (Mr. F!), because the mini-palaces he built were poorly constructed, or because he only intended to make money, not hurt the US? We're going to try to answer these questions about George Sr.'s possibly treasonous and actually inferior homebuilding from the standpoint of political philosophy, the study of how individuals relate to governments. In particular, we're going to explore the nature of the duties we may owe to our government with a focus on the duty to not commit treason against one's own country. We're especially concerned with how George Sr. may have failed to fulfill this duty and to what degree he failed to do so.

"Do You Know How They Punish Treason?"—First Time . . .—"I've Never Heard of a Second!"

The fact that treason is the only crime defined in the U.S. Constitution highlights the significance of George Sr.'s alleged crime, no matter how light it may be. Article III, section 3 defines treason in the following way: "Treason against the United States, shall consist only in levying War against them, or in adhering to their Enemies, giving them Aid and Comfort." The constitutional definition gives us several key concepts to focus on when evaluating whether someone committed treason. Citizens can commit treason in two ways: Either by levying war against their country or by helping an enemy. We'll call the first type of treason aggressive treason and the second type, in accordance with the defining behavioral trait of the Bluth family, passive-aggressive treason.

Aggressive treason is clear enough. It involves trying to bring down the state. Fortunately, nothing throughout the three seasons of *Arrested Development* ever indicates that George is a revolutionary hell-bent on bringing down the American government. So, the question at hand is really whether George's actions amount to passive-aggressive treason.

Passive-aggressive treason is the kind of treason that involves benefiting or helping out some group or state that is hostile to your homeland. What does this entail? It could involve giving an enemy of the state "aid and comfort," something that might show that you adhere to their cause. But adhering to a cause and aiding a cause aren't always the same thing. For example, Lindsay's charitable endeavors involve raising money for many causes, including the anti-circumcision group H.O.O.P. (Hands Off Our Penises) and the inconsistent triad of "No More Meat," "No More Fish" and "More Meat and More Fish." She definitely provides aid, however inept, to each organization without adhering to, supporting, or standing by any of the causes. Alternatively, you can support a cause or country without ever benefiting it. Gob manages to support the cause of the Magician's Alliance while simultaneously hurting it by inadvertently revealing the secrets to many of his magic tricks.[1]

Actions against one's country that are analogous to Lindsay's and Gob's don't seem to fully capture the idea of treason spelled out in the Constitution. It's possible to provide aid and comfort to an enemy without adhering to their cause, and it's possible to adhere to their cause without providing any aid and comfort. So, adhering to a cause and supporting an enemy with aid and comfort are two different things. This means we shouldn't understand passive-aggressive treason as just providing aid and comfort to an enemy.

Where does this get us? Well, we can see that unambiguous cases of passive-aggressive treason involve at least three elements. First, there has to be an enemy of the state. If a state doesn't have any enemies, this type of treason is impossible. There's no rival cause to support. Second, the alleged criminal must support or stand by that enemy. This is how the alleged traitor *adheres* to the enemy. Finally, committing passive-aggressive treason requires providing some kind of comfort or assistance to that enemy. Taken together, these three elements—an enemy, support of that enemy and providing aid or comfort to that enemy—make up the three parts of passive-aggressive treason. With this in hand, let's look at the case against George Sr.

A Company Whose Founder May Be on Trial for Treason: The Case Against George Sr.

Saddam Hussein was our enemy. Regardless of the nuances of who counts as an enemy (perhaps the Sitwells? Lucille 2?), Saddam fits the bill. We waged war with Saddam twice, placed sanctions on his government for over a decade, and he long had ambitions of creating weapons of mass destruction (WMDs). If Saddam wasn't our enemy from the first Gulf War to the end of the second, *no one* would be. So, if an American supported Saddam during that time, he or she supported an enemy. Strike one.

George Sr. and the Bluth Company certainly had some sort of relationship with Saddam. He had his picture taken with Saddam in 1998, during the sanctions imposed between the first and second Gulf Wars. In the picture, Saddam's apron is embroidered with a message that betrays his character: "You'll take it the way I make it." When the Bluth boys arrive at one of the model homes in Iraq, the Saddam look-alikes recognize the Bluth name and expect them to fix the air conditioner. All of this displays a level of familiarity that implies at least some degree of repeated interaction with Saddam's regime. While it's unclear whether George Sr. in fact supports the causes of the regime, he clearly stood by them economically. Because Saddam still owed George Sr. money, George Sr. kept documentation of his interactions with Saddam H. (in the H. Maddas cooler). This demonstrates George Sr.'s vested interest in the survival of Saddam's regime. While such an interest might not constitute outright support, George Sr., given his demonstrated greed, probably wouldn't want the United States to succeed in toppling Saddam's regime. In this sense, George Sr. stood by Saddam's regime. That's strike two.

Now, the Bluth homes in Iraq certainly weren't "solid as a rock," but, even if the air conditioning didn't work, they surely provided some comfort. The model homes housed the Saddam look-alikes, and maybe even Saddam himself (as suggested by the epilogue in the penultimate episode 'Exit Strategy'). The home also hid a WMD, albeit a fake one (Homefill brand, like all other model home accoutrements) planted by one wing of the CIA. But what if Saddam had succeeded in making a real weapon of mass destruction and we had actual evidence of it, rather than a picture of Tobias's balls (see Chapter: 14, "Bunkers and Balls")? The secret room would have been a good hiding place. The CIA agent on the ground certainly didn't know about it, and Michael Bluth lived in a similar house for three years before discovering his own secret room that served as the hiding place for Tobias's bodybuilding magazines. That's strike three. The facts add up, and since George Sr. isn't the umpire of this company softball game, he probably committed passive-aggressive treason.

"He's Guilty, Michael, of Medium to Heavy Treason": The Degrees of Treason

Some cases of passive-aggressive treason are worse than others. Helping North Korea maintain an active nuclear weapons program seems worse than building mini-palaces in Iraq that barely stay together. So you probably can commit treason to varying degrees. Fortunately, by distinguishing the three elements of treason, we already have the tools to make sense of the severity of treason in George Sr.'s case.

We suggest that the degree of treason corresponds to how bad the act is along each of the elements in the constitutional definition: (1) the threat posed by the enemy, (2) the extent to which the traitor adopts the enemy's cause, and (3) the amount of aid and comfort provided to the enemy. We've already said that Saddam counts as an enemy of the United States, but, without grinding any political axes here, if Saddam only had Homefill WMDs then he may not have posed much of a credible threat to U.S. citizens. On this metric, George Sr.'s helping out Saddam's regime remains pretty light.

What about the other two conditions? If George Sr. had the destruction of the United States in mind when he built mini-palaces for Saddam, things would be pretty bad. That would definitely fulfill condition (2). But if his behavior throughout the series is any indication, George Sr. is primarily motivated by making money (Caged Wisdom, Cornballer, the Bluth Banana Jail Bars, cheap houses, and on and on) and base feelings of jealousy. After all, he sold out his twin brother, Oscar, so he could be with a wife he doesn't seem to care about all that much. Moreover, if the mini-palaces he built actually aided Iraq in hiding WMDs *or* housed prisoners of war *or* were torture facilities, this would take George Sr.'s treasonous acts to a whole other level because it would fulfill condition (3). None of those things happened. It's not like George Sr. and Saddam were making and finishing each other's sandwiches. At most, the homes provided an occasionally comfortable place to stay for a few Saddam look-alikes.

No matter how you cut it, on our interpretation of the law, George Sr.'s treason was quite light. Despite its *light* qualification, George Sr. committed treason against his country by building model homes, which aided an enemy. Just as he failed to be loyal to his family, George Sr.'s actions were disloyal to his country. The facts of the case bear this out. But political philosophy isn't just interested in whether a particular act fails to meet the letter of the law. It's also concerned with whether we ought to follow the law in the first place. Yes, George Sr. technically committed light treason, but why is that a bad thing? In order to determine why it's bad that George Sr. commits treason, we need to look at why he has obligation to be loyal to his country.

"We Do Need to Stick Together Like a Family on This": Why Treason Is Wrong

Sometimes philosophers make easy questions seem hard. Didn't we just show that treason involves supporting the enemies of the state? Enemies—like Saddam—who wouldn't lose any sleep if the United States was wiped off the face of the earth! We know why mass murder is wrong—it kills a lot of people. And presumably, helping a dictator hide WMDs would make someone partly responsible for mass murder if the WMDs were ever used. However, being a murderer, even a mass murderer, is different than being a traitor. If you help Saddam develop and maintain WMDs and he blows up his own people, you have a hand in the mass murder. By itself, however, that terrible deed doesn't make you a traitor to your own country. Helping hide the WMDs would amount to *treason* only if Saddam threatens your homeland. The defining characteristic of treason is intending harm to your country or compatriots. So, the wrongness of treason must depend on some special duty or obligation George Sr. has to his country or fellow citizens. Philosophers have come up with a lot of theories about why we have an obligation to our fellow citizens or country, and these theories can roughly be sorted into one of two umbrella categories: instrumental theories and relational theories. Since each type of theory provides a different kind of explanation as to why we have the obligation, they provide different standards to use for assessing George's dealings with Iraq.

The Instrumental Approach

According to instrumental theories, the reason we should all support our government, and the reason why the government can demand obedience, has to do with the benefits a government provides that cannot be secured any other way. On this general approach, the government is a tool that we can use to reach our goals. Governments are particularly good at helping us secure certain goods that are hard for individuals to get but which help everybody; for example, no individual can secure our borders. Just look at Buster. He couldn't get a bird out of the house without causing damage or even get over a medium-sized wall during his army training. There's no way he could protect the U.S. borders. Whether individually or collectively, citizens have very good reasons to support any government that can protect them and help them get what they want.

In addition to securing things we need, governments may be in a better position to discharge moral duties that would otherwise depend on personal contributions. If the many unworthy causes Lindsay stumps for are any indication, private efforts to meet moral duties sometimes fall short. After all, people would rather donate to the imaginary disease T.B.A. than the very real Graft-Versus-Host which is affecting Tobias. Governments potentially do better in both identifying the real problem areas—things other than T.B.A.—and channeling resources to the real problems.

In addition to channeling resources, governments can secure rights better than individuals. We probably have a duty to ensure that people aren't discriminated against in the workplace. While individuals can exert some social pressure to prevent discrimination, the U.S. government can impose stiff penalties, enough to "redo a kitchen," in the process safeguarding the workplace for homosexuals against the antics of people like Barry Zuckerkorn. In order for the government to provide these services, however, it needs to have the power to keep us in line.

So, on the instrumental approach, the basis of our political obligations centers on the fact that government or political institutions are the most efficient means for securing public goods, like national defense, or meeting our moral duties, like charity or securing basic rights. What's bad about treason is that it attempts to undermine or subvert this efficient mechanism. This approach to obligation, however, doesn't provide a strong basis for criticizing many actions that fall under our understanding of passive-aggressive treason. While building model homes in Iraq may aid the enemy, it doesn't seem to provide any direct support for Saddam in a way that undermines or threatens the ability of the United States to secure public goods or meet moral duties. On the instrumental account, George Sr. violates the legal definition of treason, but he does so in a way that isn't particularly problematic. That is, he aids the enemy in a way that doesn't undermine the basic projects that generate our duties or obligations to our government and fellow citizens.

As George Sr.'s case brings out, if the basis of our special obligation to our country and compatriots follows from the fact that our government can serve as an efficient means to our moral ends, then most acts that meet the legal definition of treason may not be as bad as non-treasonous crimes. Whether buying Gob a yacht with company money or lining the walls of the banana stand with cash, the Bluth Company consistently keeps money off the books and tries to hide it from the government. Unlike building the mini-palaces in Iraq, withholding money owed to the government directly impacts the government's ability to secure public goods or safeguard rights. By withholding taxes, the Bluth Company fails to contribute to the country's collective projects. Without money, the government can't work to secure our borders or secure the rights of minorities in the workplace. These ends, which make government worthwhile and provide the basis for our political obligation, require contributions to the government. On the instrumental account, hiding that money in the banana stand (much less burning it) seems worse than committing passive-aggressive treason by building mini-palaces in Iraq.

The Relational Approach

The second approach to political obligation explains why Americans have a unique obligation to fellow Americans in terms of the nature of the special relationship we have with one another. The relational approach extends the idea of family obligations to the community of the state. Rather than look at the kinds of things the government can do (like the instrumental approach), the relational approach locates the basis of our obligations to fellow citizens in the nature of our relationships with one another.

Think about why there are things that you should do for your friends that you don't have to do for other people. Friends help each other out. Friends have a shared past. Friendship is a bond where each person is willing to say, "It really matters to me how well my friends are doing." Proponents of the relational approach think of our duties to our fellow citizens like this. Our duties toward one another depend on our shared history, culture, and the special bond that makes you want to see the USA win at the Olympics. Similar to Michael's "Family First" motto (and also very different from breakfast being the most important thing), our relationship to other Americans is kind of like our relationship to family. We didn't choose it, but we went to the same kind of schools, grew up in the same kind of neighborhoods, and these kinds of things create the bond of civil society. What's wrong with treason on this account has less to do with my relationship to the state and more to do with committing acts that hurt my political community. Aggressive treason is like stabbing your friend in the back (perhaps literally) and passive-aggressive treason is like breaking a promise to your friend by hanging out with someone who doesn't want you to be friends.

The relational approach better captures part of what's wrong with *treason*. Again, what distinguishes treason from other crimes is its reflexive nature: It harms the traitor's homeland. If the basis of our duties to our fellow citizens depends on our common bonds, we should blame those actions that threaten or go against that bond. Part of what's wrong with treason is the message expressed by the action. Think about when Michael ran the father/son triathlon at the Church and State Fair with his (possible) nephew Steve Holt (!). Michael's actions betrayed his son and brother, damaging the bonds that tie family together. He denied his son the chance to run the course with him, which made George Michael feel like less of a man. It also undermined Gob's chances to bond with his (possible) son. That's what made his actions wrong, even if everything worked out in the end.

As fellow citizens, we're in this thing together; supporting an enemy, even if the country ends up okay, expressly rejects the spirit of communal endeavor. George Sr., by trading with Iraq in the first place and subsequently trying to cover it up, performed actions that undermined the spirit of community that makes legitimate government possible. This is what makes George Sr.'s doing business with Saddam's rogue regime a huge mistake and blameworthy in the eyes of not only the law, but also the community.

"I've Made a Huge Mistake"

So, George Sr. committed light passive-aggressive treason. He violated laws by trading with Saddam and giving aid and comfort to an enemy of the United States. What should we make of it? On one hand, if our allegiance to a government depends on how well it helps us secure public goods or discharge moral obligations, then George's passive-aggressive treason doesn't seem so bad. Many of his other illegal activities do more to undermine the efficient running of the government. On the other hand, if our duties are based on the bonds of fellowship shared by citizens of a state, the intent and deception involved in building the mini-palaces serve as a much bigger insult. He broke the laws of *his* country siding with someone hostile to *his* nation. Even if his action did not lead to a direct threat against the United States, we should blame George Sr. for willfully flouting the community of which he's a part. If you're going to break somebody's heart, at least be honest about it.

NOTE

1. Sorry, we meant illusions.

"I'VE MADE A HUGE MISTAKE"

George Oscar Bluth Jr. and the Role of Error in Character Development

*Christopher C. Kirby, Jonathan Hillard,
and Matthew Holmes*

And since it is rare for a man to be divine . . . in the same way a brutish person is also rare among human beings . . . but some cases [of the latter] occur that are due to disease or *arrested development*.

—Aristotle (384–322 BCE) *Nicomachean Ethics*[1]

Everyone knows the Bluth family is full of eccentric characters, each notable for his or her peculiarities and foibles, and all suffering from some form of arrested development. Standing out among this motley crew of misfits is George Oscar Bluth Jr.

(or Gob, as the family calls him), who is perhaps the most morally ambiguous character of the series. Whether the context is one of his numerous and quite public career failures, a romantic indiscretion, or a botched attempt to show up his brother Michael, the one line that we have come to expect most from Gob is "I've made a huge mistake."

While nearly everyone in the family utters the words, Gob has made them his catchphrase. Whereas other characters tend to learn from their mistakes, Gob never does. Gob is thus an interesting case study in the role of error in the development of "moral character." Someone who fails to do what is right in a *particular* situation might not be held morally blameworthy by others if that action seems out of the ordinary (or, "out of character") for that individual, or if he or she appears to learn a lesson from the experience (or, "builds character"). But, what about Gob, who never seems to learn his lesson? Aristotle (384–322 BCE), the grandfather of character-based ethics, offers us only a little help when he writes, "When the injury takes place contrary to reasonable expectation, it is a misadventure. When it isn't contrary to reasonable expectation but does not imply vice, it is a mistake."[2] While any reasonable person could likely predict the injuries caused by Gob's assorted goofs and gaffes, how do we determine whether these actions imply vice or simply exhibit "mistakes?" A closer look at some of the major contributors to this character-based moral philosophy may help us answer this question and reveal both the comedic and philosophical value of Gob's character.

"And I'm Not Afraid to Make Mistakes. Or Have You Forgotten to Read This . . ."[3]

Let's consider one of Gob's first notable foul-ups (is it correct that this is Gob's FIRST notable foul-up?) (from "Key Decisions") in light of Aristotle's thoughts on character. Trying to further his career as a professional magician, Gob proudly announces during Marta's interview for *Acceso Mexico* that he plans to stage an escape from the prison where his father is held.[4] This single act isn't enough for Aristotle to claim that Gob lacks *arête*, or moral excellence (despite it being so inconsiderate to Marta). Many moral philosophies look to the intentions or to the consequences of a particular act as the litmus test for determining moral worth.

Aristotle, on the other hand, believed that intentions and consequences were only relevant for determining someone's *hexis*, or moral "disposition." According to Aristotle's formula, one should aim to fine-tune one's moral disposition through a rational activity of avoiding extremes because cultivating this kind of disposition could lead to human flourishing, what he called *eudaimonia* (often translated as "happiness").

Thus, only by examining a series of actions can we make an Aristotelian judgment of Gob's moral character. His actions and intentions are only important insofar as they apply to his moral disposition. According to Aristotle, any virtuous trait, such as courage, rests between two extremes—in the case of courage, these would be foolhardiness (an excess of courage) and cowardice (a deficiency). The evidence suggests that Gob has strayed very far from the path of flourishing. Once in jail, Gob's scheme requires passing a key through his digestive system (quite an impressive trick, considering we are never told how Gob got his hands on a key that presumably can break him out of his cell in the first place, though it was fun watching him attempt to swallow the key). Instead, he discovers he didn't account for some of the realities of prison life:

> **Gob:** Is there a private bathroom nearby?
> **George:** You're looking at it.
> **Gob:** No, no, no. I can't use that. I need privacy. Yeah, I've always been that way. I can't go without privacy. I can't pass this key without privacy.

George: Well, I could ask the guys to leave, but, uh . . . you know, they've been locking the doors lately. I don't know.

Gob: I've made a huge mistake. ["Key Decisions"]

Of course at this point we may say: "Only now that you can't use a private bathroom do you realize that you made a mistake?! What about recognition of the injustice performed against Marta, or against Michael by making him an accomplice to this exploit by taking her to the "Daytime Desi" award show?!" But, Aristotle makes an important distinction between an active wrong and a wrong committed unintentionally.

Those we might label "unjust," Aristotle tells us, must have some grasp of the injustices they have committed, and Gob clearly lacks this. However, we see Gob utter his line again later, after proudly telling Marta that he wants to stay with her and that they will be together for a long time. She leaves, and he immediately admits the error. In this instance, it seems, he *has* knowingly deceived her. His boastful nature has once again landed him in the position of admitting a "huge mistake." He can't seem to find the Aristotelean mean of "truthfulness" and "proper pride" between these two extremes.

In the next episode, called "Marta Complex," we witness a hilarious love triangle (or perhaps a love rhombus, if you include Buster's crush) escalate after Michael makes a toast to the family.[5] Michael embeds a proclamation of love to Marta within this speech. She is moved and realizes *she* has made a huge mistake, for it is actually Michael she loves. Gob unwittingly reports this to Michael the next day:

Gob: Michael.
Michael: Hey.
Gob: Great speech last night.
Michael: Really? What did it inspire you to do, kill somebody?
Gob: Getting there. Marta's cheating on me.
Michael: What?

Gob: Yeah. Can you believe that?

Michael: That's crazy, Gob She's not a cheater. If she were to cheat, I'd like to think she'd cheat . . . you're the cheater.

Gob: That's how I know all the signs. Last night she was all distant and weird. Wouldn't let me make love to her on Mom's bed. I don't even want to tell you what she wouldn't let me do to her in the car. And then today, I overhear her talking on the phone about somebody, all super silently, all in Spanish.

Narrator: In fact, Marta was on the phone with her mother talking about Michael.

Marta: *No es el* Gob *el que yo quiero. Es el hermano.* (Computer beeping.)

Marta: *Hermano.* (Subtitle: The brother)

Gob: And she kept using this guy's name like, "Hermano."

Michael: Let me tell you something, Gob. We're going to track this Hermano down, okay? And we're going to nail him. Because if anyone's going to go out with that girl, it's going to be one of us.

Gob: Right. Me.

Michael: And I'm okay with that. ["Marta Complex"]

Gob is livid. Yet, this makes little sense, considering that he's been unfaithful all along with various women, including "Legs," the bottom half of the woman from the "saw-a-lady-in-half illusion" in the episode "Storming the Castle." These actions, in connection with the many other vices that Gob demonstrates, would be enough for Aristotle to deem him wicked, not because of any particular act, but due to Gob's failure to use his rational faculties toward flourishing. He does not have the disposition to embody the excellence of character that Aristotle called justice, which he described as

> that in virtue of which the just man is said to be a doer, by choice, of that which is just, and one who will distribute either between himself and another or between

two others not so as to give more of what is desirable to himself and less to his neighbor, but so as to give what is equal in accordance with proportion; and similarly in distributing between two other persons."[6]

Gob's inability to balance his responsibility for the wrongs he has committed and his desire to seek revenge against those who have wronged him (for example, his obsession with finding "Hermano") are precisely what make him unjust. Aristotle may not find Gob to be a morally praiseworthy individual, but we can appreciate his character for both comedic and philosophical reasons. His "huge mistakes" are often times incredibly hilarious. They also set good examples for the kinds of behaviors that we should avoid if we wish to cultivate our own excellence, our own *arête*.

"Nobody Makes a Fool out of Our Family without My Help."[7]

While Gob is one of the most endearing characters on *Arrested Development*, the terms of his endearment are those of the fool. It's *because* he's a buffoon that Gob is such a great character— some of the funniest parts of the show are those moments of realization when Gob utters his famous catchphrase, "I've made a huge mistake." We love these moments, frankly, because, we don't have to deal with them. We just get to watch as the high jinx and hilarity ensue, knowing all the while that everything will be fine at the end of the half hour (for us, anyway).

In the real world, we're far less forgiving of people like Gob. We're usually willing to look past understandable mistakes, but we tend to blame others when their actions are obviously unwise. We feel that they should've known what would happen when they acted. Of course, when Gob makes a mistake, it's always incredibly obvious (For instance, everyone knows he should never have given up animation rights to

Mr. Bananagrabber®). No matter how much we may like Gob as a character, the truth is that if we had to deal with him in real life, we would think he was a jerk (because, well, he *is*).

Since Gob doesn't fare well with Aristotle, let's consider another philosopher who might come to Gob's defense. David Hume (1711–1776) was a very influential thinker in the field of epistemology (the study of knowledge and how people know). According to Hume, people have two kinds of thoughts: impressions and ideas. Impressions are the things that we experience—sights, sounds, tastes and smells, as well as feelings and emotions. Ideas are the things we think about—they are the rational concepts we use to make sense of our experiences, like the idea of a circle, or the principle of addition, or even the concept of justice. But where does morality fit? Well, when we blame people for making obvious mistakes, we're putting morality in the category of rational ideas. We're saying that being moral is a matter of being rational, and so by acting in a way that is clearly unreasonable, a person is acting immorally. Gob should know better, and that's why we consider him a jerk.

But Hume would disagree with this line of thinking. In his first book, *A Treatise on Human Nature*, Hume points out that being immoral and being irrational are two totally different things. Most of us have at some point discovered that reason can justify some very immoral actions. Hume makes this point in a famous line from the *Treatise*, "'Tis not contrary to reason to prefer the destruction of the whole world to the scratching of my finger."[8] If we were to find out that Gob would rather see the whole world fall apart than have two of his fingers cut off by Buster during a magic trick (illusion . . . *master*) in "Sword of Destiny" and subsequently reattached incorrectly by an incompetent doctor, we could call him selfish and immoral, but not irrational. Hume points out that as long as the conclusion doesn't involve a misunderstanding or miscalculation, it is perfectly rational—no matter how reprehensible it might be.

And if it's possible to be rational and immoral at the same time, then morality can't be based on rationality.

But if morality isn't based on rationality, what's it based on? Hume believed that impressions provide the answer. We experience morality more like a feeling than an idea. For example, when we see the attack ad that Gob made for George Michael's campaign for student president in "The Immaculate Election," we don't have to reason out whether or not the ad is bad. As soon as Gob's voice-over points out that the frontrunner, Steve Holt (!), "doesn't even know who his father is" (it's Gob), we immediately get the feeling that he has crossed the line. According to Hume, we get that feeling from our "moral sense," the part of our personality that generates the feeling that something is good or bad. This moral sense isn't rational. It reacts before we get a chance to think about the situation. Consider how you would immediately pull your hand away from the flesh-searing Cornballer, only thinking about your reaction after it had occurred. Our moral sense works in the same immediate way. It's part of how we perceive a situation. It isn't the result *of* seeing a situation and then reflecting on it.

This, however, doesn't mean the moral sense is irrational—at least, not in the sense that it violates reason. The moral sense is like anger. We can feel angry about the Cornballer without any reasoning whatsoever, so anger isn't based on reason. But it isn't *irrational* either (that Cornballer shouldn't be on the market at all!). It's perfectly reasonable to be angry with the Bluths for making that stupid device. In both anger and morality, the feeling we have is *nonrational*—it might be influenced by reason, but isn't dependent on it.

So what does this mean for Gob? Do his mistakes still make him a bad person by Hume's estimation? Not necessarily. Remember, morality isn't a matter of being rational, so making unreasonable or inadvisable choices isn't automatically morally wrong. In fact, Gob's mistakes have the potential to make him *more* morally mature. One difference between ideas and impressions is that, while reason and ideas can be taught in a classroom, impressions like emotions and morality can be refined only through experience. Sure, you can learn the arguments for why murder is immoral, but you won't really *feel* that it's wrong unless you have some experience of the value of human life. So every mistake that Gob makes is really an experience that can help refine his moral sense. In the episode "Forget Me Now," for example, we get a rare glimpse of Gob growing as a character when, after avoiding his son Steve Holt (!) throughout the episode, Gob is approached by Steve, who thinks he's accidentally slept with his cousin.

> **Steve:** I've made a huge mistake.
> **Gob:** I know the feeling—I had you. [They embrace.] I'm your father, Steve Holt! I can't hide from it anymore!
> **Steve:** I won't forget this . . . Dad! ["Forget Me Now"]

This touching moment was only possible because Gob had experienced so many failed attempts to win his own father's approval that when he saw that his son needed him, Gob finally grew into a more mature man, a true father figure for poor Steve Holt (!).

But does this mean that his constant mistakes make Gob a good person? Again, not necessarily. Mistakes are only valuable if we learn from them, if we use them to refine and mature our moral sense. In Gob's case, one of the things fans know they can count on is that he will *never* learn from his mistakes. In fact, Gob seems to actively try to keep himself from developing any moral sense. After reconciling with his son in the scene just mentioned, Gob, realizing he's becoming a more responsible human being, promptly decides to take one of the pills he carries for protecting the secrets of his magic tricks (illusions!).

> **Steve:** I won't forget this . . . *Dad*! [He exits]
> **Gob:** I will . . . [He swallows a Flunitrazepam pill] I will.

Perhaps even David Hume can't defend Gob's actions. His stubborn refusal to learn from his mistakes means that Gob will never cultivate his dormant moral sense. In the end, Gob may very well deserve to be called a bad person. It isn't because he makes mistakes, but rather, because of his arrested moral development. On the other hand, it's that very quality that makes him so much fun to watch.

"... She Keeps Saying That God Is Going to Show Me a Sign. The ... Something of My Ways. Wisdom?"[9]

Whether one accepts Aristotle's claims about reason and moral disposition, or Hume's regarding impressions and moral sense, the bottom line seems to be that becoming a good person involves the practical application of some sort of knowledge. Two contemporary philosophers in particular—Alasdair MacIntyre and Joel Kupperman—have taken up this insight and carried the character-based moral tradition we have here explored into the twenty-first century.

In 1981, MacIntyre published a book that helped revive the study of character-based ethics in the English-speaking world, titled *After Virtue*. Exploring how the notion of virtue could survive the criticisms that many older theories (such as Aristotle's and Hume's) had received, he wrote,

> When Aristotle speaks of excellence in human activity, he sometimes though not always, refers to some well-defined human practice: flute-playing, or war, or geometry. I am going to suggest that this notion of a particular type of practice . . . is crucial to the whole enterprise of identifying a core concept of the virtues.[10]

MacIntyre has a robust definition of practice: A practice is a complex, cooperative enterprise that is established socially and promotes human welfare by achieving particular goods toward which only it could aim (C'mon!). For instance, pulling a coin out of White Power Bill's "dirty ear" isn't a practice under MacIntyre's view because it is a singular act whose end (which is presumably entertainment, *not* getting stabbed) could be attained by any number of other acts. Magic, on the other hand, *would* be considered a practice because it is an endeavor that requires cooperation among a community (such as The Magician's Alliance) and requires a certain level of commitment both in order to become an initiate and to continue its traditions. Though we may deem folks like Tony Wonder and the other members of Gob's former alliance ridiculous, their commitment to the *institution* of magic itself makes them, and not Gob, good magicians. They are "practitioners"; Gob isn't.

Of course, no one needs the help of a philosopher to determine why Gob is a bad magician. What we are really concerned with is whether this says anything about his moral status. MacIntyre would say it does. He claims "character" is something like a "unity" in a human life that emerges when the various practices one is involved in, begin to cohere. Kupperman agrees and calls this type of human life an "integrated" one, and he sees this as being the source of someone's moral integrity. In his words,

> Sense of self is crucial to happiness, the degree of which, in turn, makes a major contribution to a good life. Beyond this, a sense of life as meaningful requires ongoing commitments or other forms of connection among the stages of life, which to be maintained in difficult situations call for a strong character.[11]

People who develop this kind of unity in their lives do so by distilling out what is common among the commitments they have toward individual practices. They give their life a unified meaning, and can tell a single "story" about themselves. This, according to MacIntyre and Kupperman, is where the definition of character resides—in one's "story" (or "narrative").

When we are able to tell such a story, we gain insight into our lives. We are able to apply our knowledge both practically and liberally, and we call this insight and this ability "wisdom."

Of course, the story that Gob would tell of himself doesn't jibe with the narrative we're all familiar with. Consider what happens when Michael confronts Gob about his indiscretions:

> **Michael:** Gob, instead of always coming to me looking for money, saying, "I've made a huge mistake," you can bail yourself out next time.
> **Gob:** [Laughs nervously] I've never admitted to a mistake. What would I have made a mistake about? ["The One Where Michael Leaves"]

Because Gob refuses to truly own up to his mistakes, he is unable to find a unity in his life that could render it meaningful. Instead, he coasts aimlessly through life on his Segway, bouncing from one questionable pursuit to the next (stripping with the Hot Cops, performing with Franklin, pimping for Nellie), committing one "huge mistake" after another because he can't commit to *any* practice at all. Gob's life, like his magic, embodies all kinds of errors, even if he does recognize a mistake here and there (whether he'll admit it or not). Sadly, Gob severs himself from wisdom as completely as a bloodthirsty seal severs a hand. Philosophy could help him, if he took it up, but there's little chance of that—and this may be the hugest mistake of all.

NOTES

1. Bk. VII Ch. 3, 1145b 27–33 [Our emphasis].
2. Ibid. Bk. V Ch. 7, 1135b 17–19.
3. "Amigos," season 2, episode 3.
4. "Key Decisions," season 1, episode 4 (Gob had mistakenly revealed an illusion to the public in "The Pilot" and had subsequently been barred from the Alliance of Magicians, an organization he founded.)
5. "Marta Complex," season 1, episode 12.

6. Aristotle, Bk. V, Ch. 5, 1134a 1–6.

7. "Switch Hitter," season 2, episode 7.

8. David Hume, *A Treatise on Human Nature* (Barnes & Noble, 2005) p. 320.

9. "Family Ties," season 3, episode 11.

10. Alasdair MacIntyre, *After Virtue.* 2nd ed. (South Bend, IN: University of Notre Dame Press, 1984), p. 187.

11. Joel.Kupperman, *Character* (Oxford University Press, 1995), p. 143.

THE COMEDY OF CONTRADICTION

Erin Fay and Willie Young

The lives of the Bluths are full of hilarious, and often immoral, contradictions. Since the hilarity may be obvious, let's turn to the philosopher Immanuel Kant (1724–1804) to shed light on the immoral part. Kant held that "If the intent of the action can without self-contradiction be universalized, it is morally possible; if it cannot be so universalized without contradicting itself, it is morally impossible."[1] He calls this the categorical imperative, and it means that lying, for instance, is unethical because it is self-contradictory. When Lucille lies, she wants others to believe her. But of course, if lying were made a universal law, then nobody would believe what anybody else said, and Lucille would lose much of her manipulative power. Thus, she must will for others to be truthful, while willing herself to lie. Because her will contradicts itself, lying is unethical.

Of course, "Liar" could be the middle name of each member of the Bluth family, who might also be pictured next to "self-contradiction" in the dictionary. *Arrested Development* is a comedy of moral contradiction that highlights the conflicts, tensions, and misunderstandings that permeate our attempts to be moral. Like George Michael, we all try to sift through the conflicting desires, messages, examples, and teachings to find a way to know what to do and who we should be. Watching the Bluths efforts go horribly wrong, pulling disaster from the jaws of success, we laugh at both them and ourselves.

Seemingly Deceptive: Lindsay's Lies

Lindsay Bluth Fünke constantly hints that her husband is gay and encourages her daughter to . . . well, Lindsay doesn't actually encourage Maeby to do much of anything. While it's pretty clear that Lindsay doesn't really get how to be moral, we might ask if she understands how to be consistent, and if so, what she *does* consistently.

With her ever-expanding wardrobe, one thing Lindsay does consistently is shop. Indeed, Lindsay is driven to desperation in her desire to shop. In "Not Without My Daughter," Lindsay sought a job as a shopgirl to pay for her addiction, a depth to which she never thought she would sink. Yet when asked how she got the clothing purchased with her earnings, Lindsay claimed to have stolen them. She lied to her family to hide her legitimate employment.

So Lindsay takes a legal job in order to support her shopping, but tells her family that the clothes were obtained through illegal means. This doesn't sound consistent; but does it make her *immoral*? Does lying make her actual work immoral? Kant believes that it does. He writes, "That action is immoral whose intent cancels and destroys itself when it is made a universal rule. It is moral, if the intent of the action is in harmony with itself when it is made a universal rule."[2] As Gob would say,

"C'mon!" What does that mean? Well, Kant is saying that what matters in an action is the reason behind it. If the reason for an action could apply to everyone, then the action itself is moral. In taking the job, Lindsay acted for a reason: to make money for shopping. Since the society in which Lindsay lives is based on exchanging labor for money and money for goods, this action is, on its own, moral; after all, everybody could consistently work in exchange for money and goods. What about her second action, though? What about lying to her family? Why would Lindsay act immorally by lying about an ethical action?

Basically, Lindsay lied because of the embarrassment that she felt about working (a real job). Lindsay's philanthropic "work" provides a clue to her embarrassment at working. She constantly strives to *appear* to be a philanthropist. She runs benefits and stages protests for causes that she doesn't truly understand, and that often contradict one another (who could forget this triad: "No More Meat!", "No More Fish!", "More Meat and Fish!"). And her support for Hands Off Our Penises (H.O.O.P.) caused repercussive lawsuits. But for Lindsay, the cause doesn't matter so much as *her* involvement in the cause. She wants to be perceived as a well-to-do woman who spends her time on charities and protests.

Kant writes, "A wealthy man is highly esteemed by his fellows because of his wealth; a needy man is less respected because of his strained circumstances."[3] For the Bluths, stealing is better than an honest day's work—after all, it's "built into the price." If she didn't steal, then "people would be overpaying for no reason." So Lindsay wishes to hide the need for employment while seeming to afford the clothing that's part of her wealthy lifestyle. Lindsay lies about working to maintain her own self-image and pride. She would rather spread an immoral untruth than lose social status by doing the right thing and telling the truth.

Lindsay is, if anything, consistently inconsistent. There's a line that Lindsay isn't willing to cross, even if she lies to her family about her actions. Although Lindsay wants her family to believe that she's stolen the clothing, she never actually steals.

Does this make Lindsay's actions moral, even as she constantly lies? Lindsay works hard to appear immoral to her family, even as she tries to be seen as a philanthropist to the public. She doesn't steal even as she claims to have stolen and doesn't cheat on Tobias while claiming that she, at some point, will. In the episode "Shock and Aww," Lindsay has a heart-to-heart with George Michael in which she shows that she actually cares for the boy. While she is a lousy mother to Maeby, Lindsay wants to appear to be a good mother for George Michael. The inconsistency of her actions shows Lindsay to be deeply conflicted and contradictory, wanting to fit in both with society and with her family. As both Michael and George Michael say, family is the most important thing (except when it's breakfast). Perhaps it's only by appearing immoral that Lindsay can feel like a true Bluth (which, since she's adopted, is harder than she thinks).

A Jealous Gob

If we wanted to figure out why the Bluths are such a mass of moral confusion, jealousy would be a good place to start. Jealousy courses through the Bluths like vodka through Lucille's veins. Michael and Gob have been forced to compete for George Sr.'s affection in every way from *Boyfights* to running the business. The jealousy of the family results from Lucille's and George Sr.'s manipulation of their children, putting them at odds with one another so as to assuage their own insecurities or failures. Lucille is jealous of Lucille 2, afraid that the latter will take the business or her children's affection (which, frankly, wouldn't be that hard). Even as an adult—sort of—Buster's still jealous of his adopted kid brother, Annyong.

Kant's discussion of jealousy ties in closely with his emphasis on the abstract character of the moral law, and it epitomizes the danger of basing morality on experience. On Kant's view, jealously grows from parents' attempts to teach their children to be good by comparing them to other children. Comparing children to other children fails to teach them the moral law; children are just taught to be better than each other. Moreover, since everyone can't be better than everyone else, a jealous rivalry requires a loser. Ultimately, jealously may lead to envy and grudges, which can be even more destructive. When we're compared to someone else and come up short, we have two options: try to become like them, or try to bring them down to our level. As Kant says, "It is easier to depreciate another than to emulate him, and men prefer the easier course."[4] Thus, the intent to make one's children good may ultimately backfire, turning the kids into Gob.

Gob epitomizes the problems with jealousy. He's constantly competing with his siblings, especially Michael, trying to prove his superiority. Gob tries to seduce Michael's girlfriends, but always misses the mark. Where Michael dates Ms. Baerly in "Shock and Aww," Gob gives new meaning to "having" the civics teacher, Mrs. Whitehead. He even tries to have a "holy trinity" with Bland, I mean . . . Ann. When he runs the company (into the ground), he constantly draws attention to the cost of his suits as a way to put others down (C'mon!). He tries to shoplift clothes from Lindsay's store (where she says she's shoplifting) just to show he's the "real magician" of the family. He is, of course, busted by a thirteen-year old on Take-Your-Daughter-to-Work Day. Gob's jealousy, though dangerous, is ultimately only a danger to himself—a "burning bush" of envy that consumes him without harming others.

Think of the Children

When no one's looking, who's always there to deceive? To act her way into the spotlight? Maeby Fünke, the daughter of Lindsay and Tobias, constantly works to get noticed.

In "Justice Is Blind," Maeby creates the alter-ego Shirley, an alleged cousin who suffers from B.S., a disease that has made the poor, imaginary schoolgirl wheelchair-bound. Maeby also fakes her way into a career as a high-powered movie executive, where people complete her homework and fetch her coffee. Maeby works tirelessly to create strife and gain attention within her family. When her mother flirts with Steve Holt (!), Maeby gives Lindsay a shirt that says *Shémale*, making Lindsay unwittingly announce that she's transgendered (a "fact" that Maeby has already told Steve). In the pilot, Maeby tries to get attention by making out with her cousin, George Michael. When this fails, Maeby gives it up as a bad idea and moves on to other schemes.

In short, Maeby is all about deceptive behavior. She tries to manipulate those around her by making her actions seem innocent and pretending to be something she's not ("Marry me!"). The only person who is on to her schemes is George Michael, who developed a crush on Maeby after they kissed. When told not to do something, she's the first to do it. In the episode "Best Man for the Gob," Maeby rejoins Dr. Fünke's 100% Natural Good-Time Family Band Solution after she realizes that her mother doesn't want to join. Like her mother, Lindsay, Maeby craves attention and is willing to manipulate others to get it. Unlike her mother, she tries to appear ethical while being immoral. She tries to set herself apart from the Bluths so as to gain attention—but her actions reveal she's much more part of the family than she thinks.

"I'm Not Sure if My Ethics Teacher Would Love It if I Cheated on My Essay"[5]

With George Michael, things become more complicated. Like his father, he wants to do the right thing. Being ethical matters to him—yet somehow, he always gets caught up in others' plots and schemes. One factor is clearly his desire to be part of the family and to be accepted. So how does a character who seeks to be ethical become such a gullible sap?

One criticism of Kant's ethics has been the abstraction of the moral law. The necessity of the categorical imperative is tied to its formal character. An act is ethical if it's what could be a rule for everyone else—regardless of what that action actually is. Because it is free of content, the categorical imperative is easily distorted; rather than doing what we think everyone *should* do, we might think we should do what everyone else *is* doing. Since George Michael grows up in a house of lies and deception, he feels incapable of being truthful and honest. He can't tell Michael the truth about his feelings for Maeby. The moral law slips into a form of conformism and groupthink.[6] While George Michael tries to do the right thing, he often takes his cues from those around him.

Going Both Ways

Arrested Development is hilarious in its characters' unconscious use of double entendre. Lines are written and delivered to perfectly capture the contradiction between what the characters intend and what they actually do. These scenes are especially funny because the characters' intentions are good—but these good intentions are crushed by complete lack of self-awareness. Because it's unexpected, double entendre often makes the show more fun than a ship full of hot seamen. Michael names his son after himself and his father—only to end up with George Michael. While trying to be a good uncle, he naively sings "Afternoon Delight" with Maeby. Tobias is proud to become the world's first "analrapist," a unique combination of an analyst and a therapist. When George Michael has a crush on his ethics teacher, Lindsay thinks he needs a mother figure and offers to "fill that role" for him at any time. It's like watching Sally Field morph into Mrs. Robinson before your eyes.

The Bluth stair car is hurtling toward hell, down the road paved with good intentions.

For Kant, moral action is all about intent: Acting on reason, out of respect for the moral law, is the only basis for ethical action. As Kant writes, "Duty is the necessity of an action executed from respect for law."[7] Actions that spring from desire or feeling have no moral worth, even if they're permissible. It might be good for Tobias to be a "leather daddy," so he can get close to Maeby, but if that's his motivation, that's not truly ethical. Morality requires submission to the categorical imperative. Our desires must be constrained, bound and chained so as to obey the commands of the moral law. We stand, for Kant, "under a *discipline* of reason,"[8] and it's when we find ourselves handcuffed, kneeling at the feet of the moral law, knowing that we deserve to be punished because we have been very, very bad—*that's* when we're moral, and discover our true humanity. Tobias, stop licking the moral law's boots, you horse's ass!

In its own unique way *Arrested Development* asks us some critical questions about Kant's approach. Is ethics really all about intention? When Michael tries to do the right thing by offering the housekeeper a ride, but terrorizes a random woman who thinks he's going to kill her, is he really acting ethically? When Lindsay takes up a philanthropic cause, but wants to dry the wetlands, are good intentions really enough? Or is some attention to what one actually does necessary?

Beyond the Never-Nude: Nietzsche's Man of the Future

More and more it seems to me that the philosopher, being of necessity a man of tomorrow and the day after tomorrow, has always found himself, and *had* to find himself, in contradiction to his today: his enemy was ever the ideal of today.[9]

Whereas Kant's philosophy strives for inner consistency so as to avoid self-contradiction, Friedrich Nietzsche (1844–1900) asks whether morality itself is a contradictory project. Writing at the end of the nineteenth century, Nietzsche's world held Kant's ethics to be the height of human achievement, and valued the freedom, respect, and disinterestedness (unselfishness) of Kant above all else. For Nietzsche, however, these values were anything but what they seemed; the very "progress" of Kant completed the decline of humanity.

First, Nietzsche reflects extensively on how our values are constructed: what's the origin of our idea of goodness? He argues that our morality is *reactive*: we develop our sense of goodness, based on what we don't want done to us, out of resentment (*ressentiment*) of those who could make us suffer. By defining their *actions* as evil, and then seeing them as evil, we develop the concept of goodness: "good" is what those who can cause suffering *don't* do. This makes inactivity—or weakness—seem to be something good; as Nietzsche writes, "weakness is being lied into something meritorious."[10] By "manufacturing" our virtues, we condemn and seek to destroy our aggressive, active nature: Not asserting ourselves becomes "patience," denial of our desire becomes "unselfishness," and not retaliating when injured becomes "forgiveness." There's something vicious in our virtue, for Nietzsche, as it demands that we delude ourselves about what's good and about who we are. Like Gob, we take the strong wine of human virtue and turn it into water.

The deeper problem with this morality is that we *can't* deny ourselves. Like George Michael's desire for Maeby, our desires and drives *need* to be expressed, whether we want them to or not. Like everything that lives, we have a will to *be*—to desire, to act, to assert ourselves (this is the root of what Nietzsche calls the will to power). When we try to suppress our aggressive instincts, we only turn them inward: Rather than make others suffer, we inflict suffering on ourselves. It's this self-destruction—the will "willing its own nothingness" that leads to what Nietzsche calls *nihilism*, the destruction of human life, creativity, and value.[11] Morality comes to contradict life—arresting our development, if you will.

The Kantian idea of freedom epitomizes the problem that Nietzsche sees: *free will* confuses us, because it makes us think that we're sovereign, independent subjects, when in fact we're obeying someone else, reacting against them, or suppressing our own desire. As we obey the values and standards of others, we become trapped in the "slave morality" that Nietzsche sees as so dangerous. Only through an act of "self-overcoming," realizing our history and the different forces that shape who we are, can any real freedom be achieved. Yet this requires creating one's own values, rather than simply following the rules of morality laid down by Kant or our society.

In many ways, *Arrested Development* exposes the sort of self-contradiction that Nietzsche highlights within our quest to be moral. Buster's courage in going to Iraq is really a cowardly avoidance of a deposition; Lucille's adoption of Lindsay is just another competition with Stan Sitwell, Lindsay's altruism is another form of self-assertion, and even Michael's "keeping the family together" seems to be, in the end, just trying to do what his parents didn't do. Our virtues, to paraphrase St. Augustine (354–430), are nothing but glittering vices.

For Nietzsche, the "self-overcoming" that will create new values can only happen if we recognize the history that makes us who we are. We are, as he puts it, "hybrids": the result of multiple, conflicting systems of value, with diverse and contradictory desires. It's only by accepting these desires, rather than denying them, that we can begin to create a new sense of who we are. Like Michael and George Michael, as they sail away from the family in the last episode, it is only by coming to terms with who we are that we can hope to begin anew. By living with our contradictions, rather than trying to suppress or deny them, we may be able to put them to a different use—a comic one, like a "gay science," to use Nietzsche's term, that opens a new future.

Contradiction and the Form of Comedy: There's Always Money in the Banana Stand

"A joke is a play upon form."

—*Mary Douglas*[12]

"I think that makes the joke on Gob."

—*Michael Bluth*[13]

Gob is the joke. His attire, mannerisms, ego, and attempted magic build a form, a caricature through which the show plays on societal expectations and norms, twisting them to draw out humor. As a comedy of moral contradiction, there's no doubt that *Arrested Development* does this building, use of form, and comedy with each character. *Arrested Development* fans, whether students of Kant, Nietzsche, or the one-armed J. Walter Weatherman, all agree that this show was just plain funny. But what defines a joke? Why do we care who tells the joke and if the situation is appropriate for humor?

Mary Douglas, a British anthropologist, writes about what makes jokes funny on a universal level. People all over the world create comedy based on the situations and societies in which they live; jokes follow patterns of social deconstruction. Douglas writes, ". . . a joke is seen and allowed when it offers a symbolic pattern of a social pattern occurring at the same time."[14] By contradicting the existing social hierarchy, a joke disrupts our expectations and lets us see things in a different light. The Bluths are built entirely as a reflection of current society; George Sr. sells bananas not for a profit, but to hide in-case-of-emergency-cash in the banana stand itself. The dominant social structure, in Douglas' words, is challenged by an alternative one: our view of the legitimate small business is undermined by its being used to conceal embezzlement. When Lucille "baited the balcony" in the episode "Queen for a Day," the form being played on is that of the societal elite. Lucille epitomizes the respected matriarch, but her manipulation shows there is not "an ounce of mother's milk" in her body. By subverting the expectations of our society, the show's jokes "destroy hierarchy and order."[15] The joke is obviously, and almost always, on Gob, but it's also on all of us. In many ways, comedy emerges from the depiction of the contradictions within the social order, undermining our sense of necessity and value. After all, who hasn't had the civics teacher?

Since the style of *Arrested Development* is spontaneous itself, the jokes have a more natural feel than those on other shows. The show begins and the audience knows, from the quips and upbeat tone of the theme, that the show is a comedy. The players are introduced, the plot is set, and the stage opens to jokes continued from previous episodes and seasons. With contradictory moments or early references come flashbacks, showing Lucille saying that she dislikes Gob, or Tobias saying that he and Lindsay had some good times (Footage Not Found). Sometimes these shots date to before the show was created, giving the show a continuous and realistic feel. In this way the show ignores normal filters and levels of control. *Arrested Development* allows each episode to live as a bubble within the whole, outside of the expected consciousness. Douglas writes, following an idea first articulated by Sigmund Freud (1856–1939), "The pleasure of a joke lies in a kind of economy. At all times we are expending energy in monitoring our subconscious so as to ensure that our conscious perceptions come through a filtering control. The joke, because it breaks down the control, gives the monitoring system a holiday."[16] By giving up our conscious perceptions of reality to the television, we are freeing ourselves from control. We are accepting humor as a reflection of society.

The narrator also builds this subconscious bubble, exposing the characters's lies and deceptive behavior to show how they contradict their self-presentation. The narrator, then, provides a literal voice of reason, through which the viewer is shown the contradictions within each character and how societal expectations are reversed. If Gob wasn't shown as a social form in the environment based in television, he would appear as nothing more than a selfish jerk. With narration, he is comedic, a man who matches the attempted sincerity of his brother and the perceived charity of his sister. Since the show is set in documentary style, this element is crafted without the laugh track or obvious pauses of the average sitcom. Thus, as even its form contradicts the standard sitcom format and sense of comedy, *Arrested Development* creates a wider range of comic material—playing not only off social order and hierarchy, but even off of the expectations and order of television itself.

According to Douglas, "The wise sayings of lunatics, talking animals, children and drunkards are funny because they are not in control; otherwise they would not be an image of the subconscious."[17] By being a comedic jerk, Gob provides an insight into society that might otherwise be missed. We can learn about what is wise, or moral, by listening to those who are funny and out of control. The control in *Arrested Development* is outside the Bluth family. The Bluths are children, talking animals, drunkards (especially Lucille). They act in ways that upset what is expected, without realizing that they're creating comedy for the outside viewer. Yet their lack of control, and their many forms of self-contradiction, may help us to laugh at the contradictions in ourselves as well.

So, whether it's Kant, Nietzsche, or comedy itself, the contradictions of the Bluths afford us insight into ourselves. The only way to learn the lessons of contradiction more thoroughly would involve J. Walter Weatherman, an accident, and a lost arm.

NOTES

1. Immanuel Kant, *Lectures on Ethics*, trans. Louis Infield (Indianapolis: Hackett, 1930), p. 44.

2. Ibid., p. 44.

3. Ibid., p. 177.

4. Ibid., p. 216.

5. "Shock and Aww," season 1, episode 14.

6. Alasdair MacIntyre, *A Brief History of Ethics* (Notre Dame: University of Notre Dame Press, 1998), p. 198.

7. Immanuel Kant, *Foundations for the Metaphysics of Morals*, trans. Lewis White Beck (New York: Macmillan, 1985), p. 16.

8. Immanuel Kant, *Critique of Practical Reason*, trans. Lewis White Beck (Upper Saddle River, NJ: Prentice Hall, 1993), p. 86.

9. Friedrich Nietzsche, *Beyond Good and Evil*, trans. Walter Kaufmann (New York: Vintage, 1989), p. 137.

10. Friedrich Nietzsche, *On the Genealogy of Morals*, trans. Walter Kaufmann and R.J. Hollingdale (New York: Vintage, 1989), p. 47.

11. Nietzsche, *Beyond Good and Evil*, p. 203.

12. Mary Douglas, "Jokes," in *Rethinking Popular Culture: Contemporary Perspectives in Cultural Studies*, ed. C. Mukerji and M. Schudson (Berkeley: University of California Press, 1997), p. 296.

13. "Ready, Aim, Marry Me," season 2, episode 10.

14. Douglas, p. 298.

15. Ibid., p. 301.

16. Ibid., 296.

17. Ibid., 296.

PART SIX

AND ON THE EPILOGUE . . .

AND NOW THE STORY OF A WEALTHY FAMILY WHO LOST EVERYTHING

Arrested Development, Narrative, and How We Find Meaning

Tyler Shores

Narrating the Bluths: "A Clear-Cut Situation with the Promise of Comedy"

With its unique pseudo-documentary style, pastiche of cut-away scenes, flashbacks, sneak previews,[1] and running narrator commentary, *Arrested Development* presents us with a rather interesting example of television sitcom storytelling. We can appreciate *Arrested Development* as a show about a wealthy—and deeply flawed—family and what happens when its cozy-yet-ennui-filled lifestyle is turned upside down. Sort of like the opposite of *The Beverly Hillbillies*. But we also understand

Arrested Development as a show about the way in which a television show tells a story.

Part of that distinctive storytelling style is *Arrested Development's* clever way of creating order from seeming chaos. Recall, for instance, the complex series of events that led to Buster losing his hand. Many things could have saved that left hand, and kept Buster en route to Iraq. If Gob hadn't given a seal the taste for mammal flesh (by feeding it cats!), and if he hadn't then released that flesh-eating, bow-tie wearing seal into the wild—and if Buster hadn't chosen that exact moment to overcome his lifelong fear of the ocean, and if he hadn't misinterpreted the warning of "watch out for loose seal" ("watch out for Lucille" should go without saying!). . . . If any one of those things had gone differently, it would have made for a much less interesting episode. In other ways, the show humorously provides us as viewers with a certain sense of assurance amidst the craziness of the Bluth family. During an especially far-out plot twist in "S.O.B.s," for example, our show's narrator offers helpful guidance from above when he remarks: "Now that's a clear-cut situation with the promise of comedy."

Looking closely at the stories that make up the developing narrative of *Arrested Development* gives us a chance to examine our own relation to narrative—how and why we relate to stories the way we do, and how we can find meaning in the world by and through stories. Narrative is a way of organizing and understanding events that makes them meaningful and coherent to us. Much like the narrator of *Arrested Development*, we impose a narrative structure on the seemingly unconnected events of our daily existence to create a feeling of progression, of *something* leading *somewhere*. In his *Poetics*, Aristotle (384–322 BCE) observes that a story cannot be just any sequence of events. Rather, it must have a beginning, middle, and an end that relate to each other. As a result, we create stories that will explain why things are the way they are, how they relate, how they begin, and how they end. In fact, the philosopher and neuroscientist

Mark Turner has gone so far as to say that narrative is "basic to human thinking"; we make sense of events in terms of how one thing leads to another, and hence the ability to understand the world in narrative is "the root of human thought."[2]

Aristotle also suggests that our stories are an important way of seeking truth because stories do more than entertain us. Our enjoyment of narrative stems from the sense of shared meaning that stories provide. Stories are told and retold because they take on a sense of timelessness and universality. For that reason we learn of our most fundamental values through stories, parables, and fables.[3] Precisely what lessons *Arrested Development* teaches is an open question. But one of the things that makes the show fascinating is its playful use of explanatory narrative. In "Burning Love," for example, when Michael asks Gob how he hurt his ankle, Gob replies that he must've hurt it "shooting hoops, or something." A cut-scene then immediately shows Gob actually hurting his ankle during his patented chicken dance, ending in a hilarious bit of chaos with both Gob and Buster screaming and wailing. So perhaps stories may give us hope that there is an underlying order to our lives. Real life, of course, is never quite so neat and tidy. Things rarely happen at precisely the right moment, we almost never get the facts in exactly the right order, and we can only ever operate with incomplete knowledge of the world, left to wonder about the stories that remain untold to us.

Since this storytelling aspect (of which the narrator is very proud, exclaiming in the episode "Spring Breakout", "now that's how you narrate a story") of the show is so much a part of its distinctive style, it also serves to remind us of an important point: that this narrative way of understanding is not simply relegated to fiction. We might even imagine that our lives are lived in narrative:

> Our knowledge of the world and ourselves is in fact shaped by narrative: We dream in narrative, day-dream

in narrative, remember, anticipate, hope, despair, believe, doubt, plan, revise, criticize, gossip, learn, hate, and love by narrative.[4]

Narrative in this way presents us with an analogy for the larger task of philosophy. When we ask questions of *why*, we are seeking the story of *what*. To be sure, the process of understanding our relation to stories and how we derive meaning from them is no small task—as *Arrested Development* narrator Ron Howard so aptly puts it in "S.O.B.s," "It was a complex situation without an easy solution"—but that doesn't mean it can't be a fun process for us along the way.

"And That's Why You Always Leave a Note": What Lessons Can We Learn From Our Narratives?

To understand things in terms of narrative also entails an act of interpretation—an act that gives meaning and form to events that we experience. What makes *Arrested Development* unique is that this interpretive function is built into the structure of the show, most prominently in the form of its narrator. The narrator might be a necessity for a viewer who is presented with an often self-deceiving (see: Lucille; Gob) or very confused (see: Tobias; Buster) cast of characters who are rarely, if ever, reliable sources of knowledge. To take one subtle yet amusing example, in "Hand to God," Lindsay half-heartedly guesses that her daughter Maeby is in Sacremende for her debate club semifinals. The narrator is quick to point out that Maeby wasn't, and that a Google search of the word "Sacremende" came up with zero results and the following helpful question, "Did you mean 'Sacramento'?" That sort of interpretive activity is built into the way in which we relate to the world, and the show's narrative makes clear the ways in which we could, or should, be asking those questions of interpretation.

Characters on the show, however, are often highly selective and self-interested in their interpretation of events. Consider the case of J. Walter Weatherman.

> **Narrator:** George Sr. had used his considerable means to stage intricate scenarios, to teach his children what he considered valuable life lessons.
> **George Sr.:** We're out of milk. I could have got it earlier if someone would have left a note.
> *(Tires screeching. Car collides with a man on the street, whose arm falls off, spurting blood. Screaming and yelling.)*
> **George Sr.:** Why?! If someone had left a note, this innocent man would still have his arm! Why?!
> **J. Walter Weatherman:** And that's why you always leave a note. ["Pier Pressure"]

George Sr.'s lessons and their "meanings" show just how far selective interpretation can be stretched. Switch to Michael and Lindsay in the present:

> **Michael:** Well, those lessons worked, didn't they? I mean, we still leave notes to this day.
> **Lindsay:** Oh, that's what that was about. I thought he was trying to get us off of dairy. ["Pier Pressure"]

George Sr. is nothing if not consistent, as he takes every advantage to reinterpret the meaning of those lessons to whatever purpose best suits his present needs.

> **Michael:** I want the guy with the one arm and the fake blood. J. Walter Weatherman. How do I get a hold of him?
> **George Sr.:** Well, he's, uh, dead. You killed him when you left the door open with the air conditioner on. ["Pier Pressure"]

How can we decide whether George Sr.'s interpretation of those events is any more or less "right" than Lindsay's?

Is either interpretation more valuable than the other, since neither portrays an accurate understanding of the events as they actually are? One of the difficulties of a narrative view of things is that we are oftentimes presented with a proliferation of possible meanings—we may quickly become entangled in different ways of understanding the same events. As Judith Butler points out: "Any one of those is a possible narrative, but of no single one can I say with certainty that it alone is true."[5]

Narrative thus presents a moral choice—given that a story can be told in many ways, there are choices that must be made about what's right to include, and to exclude. When we tell the stories of our own lives, how do we justify ourselves, and the choices we make in the telling? Do we paint a truthful picture of our story to ourselves and others, or do we simply tell the story we want (and perhaps wish) to be true? Fortunately, the show's narrator provides us with those deep psychological insights rather handily, such as in "Hand of God": "Michael had always thought of himself as that great a guy. The kind of guy who could raise someone else's baby . . . But he wasn't." For us, truthfulness can be a tricky thing when we're talking about something as personal as the story of our own lives—and what we tell of ourselves, both to ourselves and to others. We have a need to make sense of our existence, and we want our lives to have a sense of purpose. We want "existential coherence"[6]— things need to fit together in a certain way and not merely be a series of random, unconnected events. The risk of such a desire, unfortunately is, "that we often deceive others and ourselves by leaving out the details of our past life that don't fit the version of the story that we want to tell."[7] But on *Arrested Development* such willful self-deception appears to be second nature for most of the characters. Notice for instance Gob while he attempts unsuccessfully to annul his marriage:

> **Gob:** Well, we did have sex . . . and I'm not a great liar.
> **Narrator:** Both things he just said were lies. ["Motherboy XXX"]

In truth, "None of us wants to tell stories about ourselves that are dull or ugly,"[8] and as a result different versions of ourselves are created through the stories that we tell. And yet, there is something intrinsically valuable in thinking about ourselves in such narrative terms—we come to realize an evolving sense of self over time, what matters most to us, and why. There's always a version of the story to be told. But how do we go about deciding the right version, for us or for others? Who would be in a position to decide whether our version of our story is right or wrong?

"And That's How You Narrate a Story"—What We Tell, What We Are

At least in the universe of *Arrested Development*, the narrator provides us with a version of the story that has an appearance of objectivity. The narrator, as both observer and interpreter, is in the privileged position to observe how "action reveals itself fully only to the storyteller . . . who indeed always knows better what it was all about than the participants."[9] When we think about it, a story's narrator can represent very different philosophical outlooks. An all-knowing, authoritative narrator can give the impression of a world that is comprehensible and inherently knowable. But, a story with a limited or unreliable narrator can suggest the unpredictability of a world that we can never fully hope to understand.

For an example of the way *Arrested Development* provides a semblance of narrative certainty, we might recall the episode "Amigos" in which the Bluths head south of the border. During a very confused conversation, the narrator comments that: "At no point were Michael and Maeby talking about the same person. And there were only four people in their group." The narration of *Arrested Development* reminds us that without comic misunderstandings the whole story of the world around us would be pretty boring. Some moments in the show typically (and in a very funny way) depict what the world looks like without that measure of narrative certainty. Even the most straightforward of communications can take dramatically different turns. Take for instance the following conversation between Gob and his then-wife:

> **Wife of Gob:** I'm in love with your brother-in-law.
> **Gob:** You're in love with your own brother.
> **Wife of Gob:** No, your sister's husband.
> **Gob:** Michael? Michael.
> **Wife of Gob:** No, that's your sister's brother.
> **Gob:** No, I'm my sister's brother. You're in love with me. Me.
> **Wife of Gob:** NO! I'm in love with Tobias.
> **Gob:** My brother-in-law?
> **Wife of Gob:** Anyways, I'm enlisting in the army.
> **Gob:** To be with your brother?
> **Wife:** No! ["Whistler's Mother"]

Just as the narrator plays a very prominent role in *Arrested Development*, we likewise must act as narrators of the stories that we live everyday: "We are constantly adopting the narrator's position with respect to our own lives and also the lives of others."[10] This storytelling impulse is ingrained in our thinking. It's a crucial part of how we identify with ourselves and others: "Our own existence cannot be separated from the account we can give of ourselves. It's in telling our own stories that we give ourselves an identity. We recognize ourselves in the stories that we tell about ourselves."[11] Stories also allow us to grapple with the mundane objects of the world—to place them in contexts that allow us to make sense of them. In this respect, narrative is "indispensable to human cognition generally."[12]

The stories we tell about ourselves result in a constant sort of self-awareness on our part. In turn, one of the characteristic qualities of *Arrested Development's* narration is its frequent use of postmodernly hip self-reference. During a segment from the poorly made television show *Scandal Makers* dramatizing George Sr.'s escape from prison (acted just as poorly by Tobias) in "Spring Breakout," Ron Howard notes:

> Due to poor acting, the burden of the story was placed on the narrator . . . but this inattention to detail was typical of the laziness the show's narrator was known for. Real shoddy narrating. Just pure crap.

If we know what bad narration sounds like, what exactly does the show suggest as better narration? Are we to take the show's narrator as any sort of indication? Perhaps. But the show's narrator often treads the line between passive observer and active participant.

In a particularly clever moment, the show pokes fun at this very predicament of narrator as participant and observer. During a confrontation between Michael and his just-fired secretary Kitty Sanchez, the local newsman John Beard (a real-life Los Angeles-based news anchor) is seen in the background, and immediately departs the scene:

> **Kitty:** Did you hear that everyone? Michael Bluth is threatening me!
> **John Beard:** I've got to get out of here. I'm part of the story. I can't be a part of the story. I can't be a part of the story. ["Missing Kitty"]

On the surface, John Beard is surely being a good journalist. On another level, it also works as the subtle posing of a question—can narrators be part of the story, and should they be? Soon after, we then see John Beard on the newscast, under the sly on-screen caption, "I" Witness: "A woman shows all during a fracas at a local restaurant"—adding "sources say" under his breath. If only the real news could be so clever. If we think of ourselves as the narrator of our own stories, this puts us in an awkward position—we're always part of the story that we tell, and yet must somehow find a way to be removed enough from it in order to tell a good story. At any given time, we find ourselves as the storyteller, the main character, or simply a background character in our or other people's stories.

The question of how we might be both observers and participants of our self-creating story is something that we may address in turning to another philosopher, Friedrich Nietzsche (1844–1900). For Nietzsche, the key is that a mindfulness of style is very important to the way in which we fashion our lives:

> How can we make things beautiful, attractive, and desirable for us when they are not? And I rather think that in themselves they never are. Here we could learn something from . . . artists who are really continually trying to bring off such inventions and feats. Moving away from things until there is a good deal that one no longer sees and there is much that our eye has to add if we are still to see them at all; or seeing things around a corner and as cut out and framed; or to place them so that they partially conceal each other and grant us only glimpses of architectural perspectives; or looking at them through tinted glasses or in the light of the sunset; or giving them a surface and skin that is not really transparent—all this we should learn from artists.[13]

As Nietzsche indicates, there is more to narration than a simple recounting; there is an aesthetic principle at work. Nietzsche wants us to be like the artist who can both see the object of his attention in the minutest details and also step back and see the bigger picture: "Where art ends and life begins; we want to be the poets of our life—first of all in the smallest, most everyday matters."[14] Much as in the telling of a story, style can become a defining characteristic of our lives if we want to be mindful of what we might call an aesthetic coherence of the way our self-narratives come together.

We see this awareness of style in the narrative selectivity of the show. In one situation that exemplifies this narrative freedom, the narrator uses an opportunity while Michael tells an especially boring story about his high school locker combination, to "channel surf" amongst the other Bluth family members:

> **Narrator:** Hey, let's see what some of the other folks are up to.
> *Crickets chirping.*
> **Narrator:** Nothing there.
> *Quiet clicking.*
> **Narrator:** Or there.
> *(Shows Buster in a hospital bed, pretending to be in a coma, while his nurse climbs in with him).*
> **Narrator:** Oh, my. Let's get back to Michael. ["Family Ties"]

In our own lives, we are accustomed to long periods in which nothing out of the ordinary seems to happen. We wish we could jump around and select only those things that are interesting to us. But, if we are to fully appreciate Nietzsche's sentiments, we must accept that even the most mundane of moments are in fact very much an essential part of the larger story of our lives.[15]

The very nature of telling our self-story is nevertheless quite difficult, as Søren Kierkegaard (1813–1855) helps us see:

> It is perfectly true, as philosophers say, that life must be understood backwards. But they forget the other proposition, that it must be lived forwards. And if one thinks over that proposition, it becomes more and more evident that life can never really be understood in time simply because at no particular moment can I find the necessary resting point from which to understand it—backwards.[16]

As Kierkegaard points out, telling the story of our lives must of necessity be an incomplete and ever-evolving undertaking.

We're always adding to the material of that story, and we're confronted with the choice of how we go about telling that story at every moment. If we agree with Kierkegaard's proposition, then this sort of narrative sense-making is a ceaseless process of backward-moving reinterpretation. We're always looking backward into our past in telling such a story because life is always moving forward in time. Likewise, that very same backward-looking approach is what rewards rewatching in a show like *Arrested Development*. It's only then that we catch some of the show's very subtlest humor—for instance, when Buster rediscovers his hand-shaped chair, "Well, I never thought I'd miss a hand so much," several episodes before he finds himself being "all right."

> **Lucille:** How's my son?
> **Literal Doctor:** He's going to be all right.
> **Lindsay:** Finally some good news from this guy.
> **George Michael:** There's no other way to take that.
> **Literal Doctor:** That's a great attitude. I got to tell you, if I was getting this news, I don't know that I'd take it this well.
> **Lucille:** But you said he was all right.
> **Literal Doctor:** Yes, he's lost his left hand. So he's going to be "all right."
> **Lucille:** I hate this doctor!
> **Lindsay:** How do we keep getting this guy?
> **Michael:** Mom, he's a very literal man. ["Hand to God"]

Perhaps the greater benefit of all of this narrative awareness, both in the show and in our everyday experiences, is that it can help us appreciate the ways in which even the seemingly most insignificant of details and moments play a greater role than we at first suspect: "Over the course of a lifetime stories may change. Characters first dismissed as 'bit players' may gain importance. Gestures or words earlier thought unimportant may, in retrospect, take on greater significance."[17] Stories define and guide us; they provide us with a sense of purpose out of which the various narrative fragments that constitute our daily lives cohere into a greater sense of meaning.

Narrative structure can also provide a sense of finality. In the show's last episode "Development Arrested," the narrator closes with "It was *Arrested Development*"—a fitting tying together from the opening credits of every episode ("It's *Arrested Development*"). That sense of finality is oftentimes one of the things that makes fiction fictional; only rarely do we have such clear-cut distinctions between the beginnings, middles, and endings of events in our lives. Even when we like to think that we're starting a "new chapter" of our lives, or that we're "turning the page" on some stage of our lives, we still face ambiguity and open-endedness.[18] In the end, narrative provides us with an analogy for life and how we might understand it, but narrative is not actually life, and life is not actually narrative—nevertheless a narrative understanding can be "an abstraction one uses . . . to understand, and predict, and make sense of, the behavior of some very complicated things."[19] Narrative helps us to connect the expected and unexpected, the intended and the accidental, the successes and disappointments, into a meaningful coherent whole by which we come to understand the selves that we are. We get a better sense of ourselves and others through the stories that we tell, and the stories that we hear—perhaps even when development of those stories is arrested.

NOTES

1. Loyal viewers will be quite familiar with the "On the next Arrested Development . . ." trailers at the end of every episode, which almost never actually happen in the following episode. Show creator Mitch Hurwitz described these in-jokes as "call forwards"—hints of events that hadn't yet happened.

2. Mark Turner, *The Literary Mind: The Origin of Thought and Language* (Oxford and New York: Oxford University Press, 1996), pp. 7, 12.

3. Anthony Paul Kerby, *Narrative and the Self* (Bloomington: Indiana University Press, 1991), p. 60.

4. Barbara Hardy, "Towards a Poetics of Fiction: 3) An Approach through Narrative," *Novel: A Forum on Fiction*, 2 (1) (Autumn 1968): 5.

5. Judith Butler, *Giving an Account of Oneself* (New York: Fordham University Press, 2005), pp. 37–38.

6. John Davenport, *Will as Commitment and Resolve: An Existential Account of Creativity, Love, Virtue, And Happiness* (New York: Fordham University Press, 2007), p. 183.

7. John Lippitt, "Getting the Story Straight: Kierkegaard, MacIntyre and Some Problems with Narrative" *Inquiry*, 50 (1) (2007): 52.

8. Ibid., p. 49.

9. Hannah Arendt, *The Human Condition* (Chicago: University of Chicago Press, 1958), p. 192.

10. Kerby p. 39.

11. Paul Ricoeur, "History as Narrative and Practice," *Philosophy Today*, 29 (3) (Fall 1985), p. 214.

12. Turner, p. 5.

13. Friedrich Nietzsche, *The Gay Science*, trans. Walter Kaufmann (New York: Vintage Books, 1974), p. 239.

14. Ibid., p. 239.

15. For an interesting study on this idea of unity in human life through narrative, check out Alasdair MacIntyre's excellent book, *After Virtue*.

16. Søren Kierkegaard, *Journals and Papers*, ed. Howard V. and Edna N. Hong (Bloomington: Indiana University Press, 1967–1978).

17. Jeannette Bicknell, "Self-Knowledge and the Limitations of Narrative," *Philosophy and Literature*, 28 (2) (2004): 406–416.

18. And as we now well know, the end is never really the end, especially in television. At the very end of that episode, we see a brief cameo from Ron Howard and a foreshadowing of things to come: "No, I don't see it as a series. Maybe a movie?"

19. Daniel Dennett, "*The Self as a Center of Narrative Gravity*," in F. Kessel, P. Cole and D. Johnson, eds, *Self and Consciousness: Multiple Perspectives* (Hillsdale, NJ: Erlbaum, 1992).

CONTRIBUTORS

Banana Stand Employee Roster

Deborah Barnbaum is an associate professor of philosophy at Kent State University. She is the author of *The Ethics of Autism*, as well as numerous articles on clinical and research ethics. She would like to dedicate her contribution in this book to her brother.

Annyong (Hello) Bluth: Which isn't a name, but the Korean word for "hello." Annyong.

George Michael Bluth: Frozen banana salesman/child.

Michael Cholbi has written a number of articles in ethics and a book about philosophical issues surrounding suicide. He satisfies his craving for bangers and mash with occasional visits to the Yellow Fang Pub.

Brett Coppenger is a graduate student at the University of Iowa whose research interests include epistemology and the philosophy of science. He has presented papers on the history of the philosophy of science, the epistemological problems of perception, and the threat of skepticism. His relentless efforts to axiomatize a system of magic have resulted in ongoing condemnation from the Alliance of Magicians, who strangely demand both to be taken seriously and not to be understood.

Darci Doll is a doctoral candidate at Michigan State University and a Lecturer at Delta College and Central Michigan University. She has published in *Pornography and Philosophy*, and her research interests include ethics and Ancient Greek Philosophy. For ease of the reader, she initially wanted to change all the gendered pronouns "he"/"she" to the feminine "she"; however, upon seeing how doing so in "The Man Inside Me" potentially alienated a broad audience, decided that it could be a huge mistake.

Michael Da Silva is a law student at the University of Toronto. He is also vice-president of the Canadian Society of Christian Philosophers and a (co)-contributor to *30 Rock and Philosophy*. He is serious and he is a professional, just like Wayne Jarvis.

Jeff Ewing is an independent scholar, focusing on Marxian thought and egalitarian alternatives to capitalism. He has been spending his spare time helping get the Bluths back on their feet, through co-producing a second Franklin album, *Franklin Attains Class Consciousness*, and the newest *Boyfights* special, *Boyfights: The Fight Against Alienation*.

Erin Faye is in her last year of studies at Endicott College, where she's majoring in liberal studies with minors in creative writing and philosophy. Ask her what she's going to do with that and she'll probably say, "Live in a box. What else?" (Secretly she wants to be a real, full-time writer. Don't tell her word's out on that dream, okay?) She's always on the lookout for Lucilles and loose seals 'cause she hears that either can be damaging to career goals—especially those that require two hands.

Paul L. Franco (Ph. D, University of Pennsylvania): Him?

Maeby Fünke is the second youngest movie executive in Hollywood, and has produced such classics as *Snow Boarding School 2*, *Gangy*, *The Young Guy and the Sea*, and *The Ocean Walker* (in production). She is also a high-school student, and has attended such prestigious schools as Openings.

Brett Gaul teaches philosophy at Southwest Minnesota State University. He is the author of articles on Descartes and G. E. Moore. Although he doesn't drive a stair car, he always watches out for hop-ons anyway.

Christopher C. Kirby is assistant professor of Philosophy at Eastern Washington University. He specializes in the history of philosophy—particularly that of ancient Greece and China—and writes on topics that connect these to American thought. He lost his hand while part of an expedition to capture a loose seal. If you have any information regarding the seal's whereabouts, please contact Mr. Gene Parmesan, Private Investigator, at 555-0113.

Jonathan E. Hilliard is a senior at Eastern Washington University. He can be found riding his Segway between bookshelves in the library. If his philosophy career doesn't pan out, his backup plan involves a certain banana stand. . .

Matthew J. Holmes is a recent graduate of Eastern Washington University. He recently abandoned his plans to enter graduate school in order to become an actor, and used his tuition money to take acting lessons from Carl Weathers. He now works on the Mr. Banana Grabber cartoon as the voice of Baby Banana Grabber.

Tim Jung is a Libra who enjoys psychoanalysis, continental philosophy, teaching, and writing. When he is not philosophizing, he works part-time teaching lessons.

Daniel P. Malloy teaches philosophy at Appalachian State University in Boone, North Carolina. He has published numerous articles on the intersection of philosophy and popular culture. Daniel is also a proud graduate of Carl Weathers's acting workshop. You going to finish that? I've got a stew going.

Rachel McKinney is a PhD student at the CUNY Grad Center. In her free time, she enjoys hunting dragons. In the future.

Douglas "Steve Holt (!)" Paletta works primarily on the nature of moral arguments and social contract theory. His recently defended dissertation, which explains how social contract arguments work, reminds him of Ann; it has a low center of gravity and you can't knock it down. (Her?)

Kristopher Phillips is an ABD graduate student of philosophy at the University of Iowa. His research interests include early modern metaphysics; specifically in Descartes and Spinoza. He has presented papers on Descartes, Hume, Berkeley, Spinoza, Leibniz, and the philosophy of biology. He has also contributed to *Coffee: Ground for Debate*. He is not, at least according to his website (http://imkristopher.com), the same person as the author of *The Socrates Café*.

Jason Southworth is an ABD graduate student in philosophy at the University of Oklahoma, Norman, and a philosophy instructor at Fort Hays State University, Hays, Kansas. His research interests include philosophy of language and philosophy of mind. He has contributed chapters to many pop culture and philosophy volumes, including *Batman and Philosophy, Heroes and Philosophy, X-Men and Philosophy, Steven Colbert and Philosophy*, and *Final Fantasy and Philosophy*. After thinking about it, he still isn't sure where to put it . . . maybe in her brownie.

T-Bone: He's a flamer (but I'm telling you this in confidence).

Ruth Tallman is an ABD graduate student at the University of Oklahoma, Norman, and an adjunct instructor of philosophy at Fort Hays State University, Hays, Kansas. She has written chapters for other pop culture and philosophy volumes, including *Heroes and Philosophy* and *Christmas and Philosophy*. She is a country music loving lady.

Tyler Shores is currently a graduate student at Oxford. He received his B.A. from University of California, Berkeley, where he created and for six semesters taught a course on The Simpsons and Philosophy (inspired by William Irwin's book of the same name). Tyler has contributed to *Heroes and Philosophy*, *Alice in Wonderland and Philosophy*, and *30 Rock and Philosophy*. He has also previously worked at Google and the Authors@ Google lecture series. Prior to this, his fondest accomplishment was the time his debate club went to Sacramende for the semifinals.

M. E. Verrochi is a graduate student in philosophy at Michigan State University. Her philosophical interests range from feminist philosophy of language to concerns regarding the intersection (and influence!) of pop culture and ways of being. In 2007, she publicly announced that she *really* is the long-lost Bluth family member, N. Bluth. Unfortunately, though supposedly nothing comes before family (except, on occasion, breakfast), she has yet to be acknowledged by the clan as one of their own. She has one thing and one thing only to say to the Bluths: *C'mon!*

J. Jeremy Wisnewski has edited *Family Guy and Philosophy*, *The Office and Philosophy*, and *30 Rock and Philosophy*. He has also written *Wittgenstein and Ethical Inquiry*, *The Politics of Agency*, and *The Ethics of Torture*. He is contemplating giving up writing, though, to take up full-time work in the Banana Stand.

Willie Young is associate professor of Humanities at Endicott College. He has written essays for *South Park and Philosophy*, *Poker and Philosophy*, and other pop culture books. He also is the author of *Uncommon Friendships* and *The Politics of Praise*. He is secretary of the Society of NeverNudes in Massachusetts, or SNM for short.

INDEX

Banana Stand Inventory